Aircraft

D1051935

Objekt

Titles in the *Objekt* series explore a range of types – buildings, products, artefacts – that have captured the imagination of modernist designers, makers and theorists. The objects selected for the series are by no means all modern inventions, but they have in common the fact that they acquired a particular significance in the last 100 years.

Series editors: David Crowley and Joe Kerr

In the same series

Factory
Gillian Darley

Aircraft

David Pascoe

REAKTION BOOKS

TL670.3
P375

To Stanley

Published by Reaktion Books Ltd
79 Farringdon Road
London EC1M 3JU, UK

www.reaktionbooks.co.uk

First published 2003

Copyright © David Pascoe 2003

All rights reserved

No part of this publication may be reproduced, stored in a retrieval system, or
transmitted, in any form or by any means, electronic, mechanical, photocopying,
recording or otherwise without the prior permission of the publishers.

Printed in Hong Kong

British Library Cataloguing in Publication Data

Pascoe, David, 1965–
    Aircraft. – (Objekt)
    1. Airplanes – History 2. Airplanes – Social aspects
    I. Title
    387.7'3'09
    ISBN 1 86189 163 6

Contents

Preface

In *La Prisonnière*, the fifth part of Proust's monumental *A la recherche du temps perdu*, the narrator plays on the piano a transcribed passage from *Tristan und Isolde*, and, as he does so, hears behind it, naturally enough, the uplifting sounds of earlier Wagnerian works; 'the eternally grateful laughter and hammer blows of Siegfried', for instance. The narrator's 'workmanlike' keyboard technique succeeds in making the phrases soar freely as birds; not the kind of winged creatures resembling, say, Lohengrin's swan but, rather, the flying machine once heard as the narrator looked into the sky over Balbec. In fact, he puts the case for the technologies of flight by suggesting that just as the birds that climb highest have the largest wings, so mankind needs 'material devices' to explore the infinity of the sky; machines such as 'those hundred-and-twenty-horsepower Mysteries' in which, admittedly, 'any appreciation of the silence of space is somewhat impeded by the powerful rumble of the engine'.[1]

Aircraft is concerned precisely with those 'material devices' Proust describes, from the flimsy contraptions of wood, wire and canvas that took to the air exactly a century ago, up to the aircraft of today, sleek machines compounded of exotic materials whose wings might touch the very edges of space. Tracing the object from

Giacomo Balla, *Sky Blue Metallic Aeroplane* (1931).

the nineteenth into the twenty-first century, *Aircraft* considers the powered, fixed wing, flying machine from several distinct perspectives: as a miracle of engineering; as a device driven by military ambition; as a product of the desire for speed; and, finally, as an inspiration for artists, architects and writers. By the time Proust was writing in the early 1920s, aircraft had conquered not only the skies, but had also, equally, overcome preconceptions regarding the uplift that might be possible through mechanical rather than artistic endeavour. Hence, Proust could suggest, in all seriousness, that technological manifestation (the noise of an air-craft in flight) and aesthetic experience (the sound of a passage of Wagner) might, in fact, be coterminous.

From the beginning, flight has been concerned as much with acci-dent as with design. Recent research undertaken by NASA – namely, the construction of a replica of the Wright Flier in celebration of the centenary of flight – has demonstrated that not simply were the Wright brothers visionary engineers, but also that they were extremely fortunate to take to the air on 17 December 1903. Despite the care taken by NASA's engineers to rebuild the machine accord-ing to the brothers' original blueprints, the imitation machine would not fly. After a fortnight of wind-tunnel tests, it emerged that the instability of the Flier was such that, aerodynamically, at least, it behaved like 'a glass marble rolling on a plate', and that a single gust of wind could have upset it disastrously. The manager of the NASA project observed that the Wrights were 'extremely lucky not to have broken their necks'. A century on, despite the appliance of aeronaut-ical advances, the reason their design succeeded, where other less risky concepts had failed, remains a matter of mystery; a question, at the very least, of art winning out over design.[2]

Within a few decades of the Wright Flier, aircraft would be celebrated not for their mysteries, but for their precision and clarity. In his celebrated manifesto, *Aircraft* (1935), Le Corbusier presented more than 100 photographs celebrating aeroplanes either in imperious flight or elegantly at rest. Dwelling on the artfully abstracted shapes of noses, wing and tails, he declared: 'Ponder a moment on the truth of these objects! Clearness of function!' His introductory essay concludes by proclaiming that 'the symbol of the new age', the aeroplane 'in the sky, carries our hearts above mediocre things' and 'has given us the bird's eye view'; a valuable gift, for 'when the eye sees clearly, the mind makes a clear decision'.[3] No doubt Le Corbusier realized that such clarity of function could only have emerged out of the uses first found for aircraft during the Great War, and perhaps this explains why, it seems, he was less exercised by the recognition of aircraft than the setting out of their general form. After all, plane-spotting has its roots in identification of the enemy, and at this point in his career, desperate for new commissions, Le Corbusier needed all the friends he could get.

So it is especially striking that in 1922 Proust should be so oddly specific in his identification of flying machinery: 'those hundred-and-twenty-horsepower Mysteries'. Proust's most recent translator offers an unhelpful gloss: 'the Mystère was a make of aircraft'.[4] It would make perfect sense if this were, in fact, the case, but this statement is incorrect, since no French model of the time was known by that name. It may be objected that the identification of this aircraft as a technical fiction is merely pedantic; but aviation enthusiasts are as alert to telling detail as any literary or textual critic, and this book is written in the spirit of both. Proust's ploy here is especially revealing, since it shows an artist fixated on a past world, nevertheless wanting to be seen to be laying claim to the 'material devices' of a new age of flight. His pretending to an extensive knowledge of aircraft perhaps suggests that when the flying machine takes to the sky, no one ever wants to be left behind.

1 Flight Engineering

Self-Propelled

As the sun set over Milan on a warm day during the International Air Week in late September 1910, the poet Filippo Tommaso Marinetti, founder and leader of the Futurist Movement, took flight over the city. The biplane in which he was a passenger was piloted by the record-breaking Peruvian aviator Jean Bielovucic, whose friend and compatriot Chavez had died in an accident a few days earlier after successfully crossing the Alps.[1] During the brief sortie, in addition to experiencing 'increasing weightlessness [and] an infinite sense of voluptuousness', Marinetti felt his chest opening up 'like a great hole into which the entire horizon of the sky flowed deliciously, smooth, fresh, torrential'.[2] Later, he would claim that this flight propelled him towards the new conception of art and language, set out in the first lines of his 'Technical Manifesto of Literature' of 1912: 'Sitting on the fuel tank of an aircraft, my stomach warmed by the pilot's head, I sensed the ridiculous inanity of the old syntax inherited from Homer. A pressing need to liberate words, to drag them out of their prison in the Latin period . . . This is what the whirling propeller told me, when I flew two hundred metres above the mighty chimney pots of Milan!'[3] The aircraft's propeller had become a component with sufficient life of its own that

A Rockwell B-1B Lancer from the 28th Bomb Wing at Ellsworth Air Force Base, South Dakota, flies over the Pyramids in 1999.

GRANDE SEMAINE D'AVIATION DE LA CHAMPAGNE (Août 1909).
PAULHAN sur Biplan cellulaire Voisin, Moteur rotatif Gnome, classé : 3ᵉ dans le Grand Prix de Champagne, 178 par 133 kil. 676 ; 3ᵉ dans le Prix d'Altitude, par 90 mètres ; 8ᵉ dans le Prix de Vitesse, en 32' 49" 4/5.

it would 'conquer the seemingly unconquerable hostility that separates out human flesh from the metal of motors'.

The machine on which Marinetti had taken his turn was common enough: a 'Box-Kite' biplane designed and constructed by the Voisin brothers, who in 1907 had established the world's first aircraft factory at Billancourt, outside Paris, making any design that a customer wanted. (A Russian prince ordered a machine with a propeller shaped like a spiral staircase – a flight of steps; a Dutch client paid for a set of wings to be grafted onto a light carriage known as a 'fly' – the design failed to take off.) Earlier they had made a glider with biplane wings and an elevator in front, similar to the configuration of the Wright Flier. Dissatisfied with its handling, however, and in an effort to obtain a measure of automatic longitudinal stability, they fitted the aircraft with a fixed biplane horizontal 'tail', between the two surfaces of which the single rudder operated. The craft, which was, in effect, a giant box-kite with an elevator and a rudder,

Louis Paulhan at the controls of his Voisin biplane, during the famous Aviation Week at Rheims in August 1909. Note the small, bullet-shaped fuel tank, on which Marinetti would squat when flown by Bielovucic during the International Air Week in Milan just over a year later.

16 *Aéroplane Delagrange. — LL.*

flew reasonably well. Its pilot sat on the lower wing with his feet protruding into a short cockpit equipped with elevators. On either side of him extended two sets of wings, upper and lower joined together by vertical struts and by four vertical panels, which, for lateral stability, combined to form symmetrical screens on each end of the wing with, at their centre, what has been described as a wide oblong 'window frame'.

Whereas the Wrights deliberately produced a machine that was entirely dependent upon the pilot's skill for its stability, the popular Voisin machine, then, was intended to be automatically stable, reducing the need for flying expertise and even allowing it to carry 'paying' cargo. Hence, above and behind the pilot, atop the small tin fuel tank, there was enough space for a single passenger, whose lower body, as indicated in Marinetti's manifesto, would have been partially shielded from the airflow by the aviator's head. Directly behind the passenger, but enclosed in the body in the

The Voisin-Delagrange Box-Kite, constructed and flown in 1907, and the first European aircraft to break the records established by the Wright brothers' Flier in December 1903.

front of which sat the pilot, was a noisy fifty-horsepower Antoinette engine driving a propeller, whose blades whirled between the outriggers carrying the tail, pushing rather than pulling the craft along. Hence Marinetti, elevated above the pilot, had before him an unrestricted vision, and could feel 'the ferocious and flushing massage of the crazy wind' full on.

The propeller is a rotating wing, generating lift exactly as a fixed wing does, but with its blades directing air backwards so that lift becomes propulsive thrust. Since wing technology in 1910 was rudimentary, the propeller, carefully crafted out of laminated and lacquered wood, was the most valuable part of the aircraft and its blades needed constant care and attention. In fact, a rag drawn into a spinning propeller's axis was sometimes enough to destroy the carefully machined edges of the blades; objects weighing only a few ounces were injurious even though, in use, the blades were designed to bear immense air pressures. At the time of Marinetti's flight, experiments were under way with other materials (copper, lacquer-impregnated linen) and technologies (metal castings) in order to reduce propeller torsion and air friction. But these developments were too heavy – and the Voisin Box-Kite machine was already rather overweight – so, in order to balance the need for lightness and strength, wood, despite its fragility, remained the preferred material for some time to come. In its curious mixture of fragility and strength, the propeller implied other antitheses, too: of the natural and the artificial; of the visible and the invisible; of component and ornament. Such properties imply that the object was more than just a cipher of civilization's mobility, but the shift it presented from stasis into movement implies a larger aesthetic problem: the relationship between the concrete and the abstract, force and flight. A French engineer wrote: 'isn't [the propeller] soul-like in its infinite smallness with respect to the whole aircraft, in its imponderability when spinning at high speeds, in its invisibility as it traverses the ether's azure?'[4] As Jeffrey Schnapp has suggested:

> The wooden propeller's intermediate position between the weight-lessness associated with the airplane's sail-like wings and the weight associated instead with the engine (in other words, between the aerial and metallic aspects of an aircraft's identity), corresponded to its location at a symbolic crossroads: right at the center of the cross formed by the airplane's wings and its perpendicular fuselage.[5]

Since now it transformed motive power into actual physical thrust, the propeller was assuming mythical proportions; as it now seemed that it alone, and not the wing, was responsible for the conquest of the air, it had come to symbolize that very visible dematerialization of matter in which the miracle of flight was thought to consist.

The propeller merged and confused sense impression. At the end of Proust's *La Prisonnière*, Marcel and Albertine hear the noise of an aircraft over Versailles: 'I had at last been able to attach the buzzing to its cause, to that little insect throbbing up there in the sky, perhaps six thousand feet above me; I could see it hum'; the propeller made noise visible.[6] This sense of the singular nature of the propeller emerged, too, in Léger's account of a visit made to the 1912 Paris Air Show in the company of Brancusi and Duchamp:

> The latter, whose character was dry and somehow unfathomable, was silently walking around the propellers that were on show. Suddenly he turned to Brancusi and said: 'Painting is finished! Who can do better than this propeller. Tell me, can you do that?' He had a great predilection for the precision of objects like those. We had too, but not in so categorical a way. Personally, I was drawn more towards the engines, to

the metal machinery, than to the wooden propellers . . . But I still remember how stunning they were. My God, they were marvellous.[7]

Notwithstanding Brancusi's awed comments, these propellers clearly revealed themselves in Léger's series known as *Contrastes de Formes*, lying behind its rotating formal combinations; then, in 1918, the propellers proper appeared in the two versions of *Les Hélices*, cramped canvases both with little space to breathe, never mind aspire to the sky. Finally, in a pair of watercolours, *La Cocarde* and *L'Avion Brisé*, in which Léger took a crashed aeroplane as the subject, the propellers are only one element among many; their characteristic curvature cannot overcome the angular disjointedness pressing into them, splintering them. Here, the

Fernand Léger, *La Cocarde* (c. 1916), one of a series of works in watercolour on paper featuring aircraft in various stages of destruction, recalled from the artist's time at the Front.

object has ceased to be an autonomous form, but simply represents a technological sublime; mechanical and the organic part of the great machine of modern civilization.

It took Léger's great friend, Robert Delaunay, to spot fully the technical and spatial possibilities of the spinning propeller, as well as of Voisin's Box-Kite, the machine that bore it so bravely. The aircraft appears first in *L'Equipe de Cardiff*, its wings reflecting sunlight breaking through a dark blue sky, broken by cloud; it is met by the hemispherical track of a Ferris wheel clearly intended to

Robert Delaunay, *L'Hommage à Blériot,* 1914, containing representations of a Voisin, an Antoinette, and several Blériots.

mark the radius of a prop; next *Soleil, Tour, Aeroplane*, in which the Voisin was partially merged into an apocalyptic array of propeller-like forms and circles of light. Finally, *L'Hommage à Blériot* features the Voisin once again, now deep red, flying in the sunset over Paris, its wings enclosed by a halo of purple and golden sunlight. This time, however, other machines are more or less prominent. A monoplane – what appears in profile to be an Antoinette – is ascending into the air to the left of the Voisin, while in the lower right eager mechanics are readying another monoplane for flight, in the direction of the disc at the dead centre of the picture. Dominating the lower half of the canvas is a beautifully shaped, giant red and mauve tractor propeller, prominent before the distinctive spindly undercarriage of what is recognizably the aircraft in which Blériot crossed the English Channel five years earlier, encircled by circles of blue, red, green and yellow.

The title of the painting is misleading since Delaunay is obviously paying homage, not to the man, Louis Blériot, '*le grand constructeur*', but to his machine, the Blériot XI, the unique design of which – rear rudder, enclosed cockpit, horizontal stabilizer and

On 23 October 1911 in North Africa, Captain Carlos Piazza of the Italian Expeditionary Force stands in front of a Blériot monoplane in which he is about to make the world's first military flight.

swivelling landing gear to permit cross-wind take-offs – had propelled its pilot so far; a machine which, in contrast to the Wright Flier, and the Voisin Box-Kite, was a monoplane, a design that air racing had proved to be faster than biplanes of similar weight and power. Its engine arrangement, too, pointed forwards; the tractor propeller pulling rather than pushing its single-minded inventor into history and, as an *homme d'affaires*, into the embrace of the military men. By the end of 1910 there were almost forty military pilots and thirty military aircraft in France; the majority of the machines were of Blériot's design. At dawn on 23 October 1911 Captain Carlos Piazza, Commander of the Italian Expeditionary Force sent to North Africa during the Italo-Turkish war, made the first operational flight in a military aircraft when, at the controls of a Blériot XI, he carried out a one-hour reconnaissance of Turkish positions between Tripoli and Azizia.[8] In February 1914, after several weeks of sustained work, Robert Delaunay completed his *Hommage*; within six months, Blériot's machines, sporting the *cocardes* of the French air force and the roundels of the British flying corps, were being employed as spotter planes over northern France, reporting troop movements, directing artillery fire and harassing the enemy. This, perhaps, is what he had in mind when he described the elements of the pictures as creating '*simultané forme*'; the circular form of the propellers contained the future.

Within the year more specialized machines were taking on a number of combat roles: *ad hoc* bombers, dropping explosive projectiles on Zeppelin sheds, or makeshift fighters, circling the battlefield, with rifles and guns welded onto pylons for sporadic use by the vigilant observer behind the pilot. Already the French ace Roland Garros was flying a Morane-Saulnier aircraft equipped with a nose-mounted machine-gun and steel deflector plates on the propeller blades to prevent damage by the arc of fire. He was forced

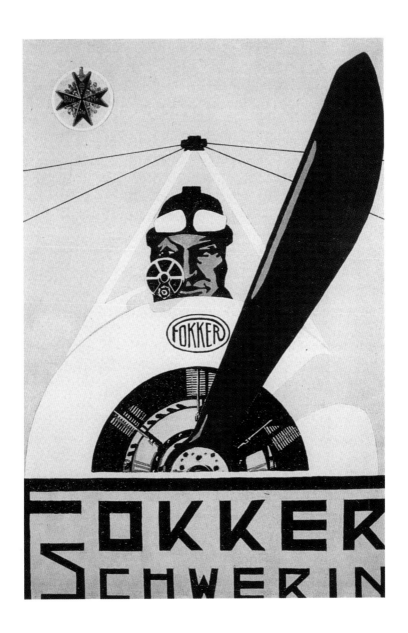

Man and machine in harmony, as the eye and the gunsight converge. A 1917 advertisement for Fokker's fighters.

down behind enemy lines in 1915, and the Germans pounced on the new weapon technology. After inspecting the deflector, Anthony Fokker, a Dutch aircraft designer working on a new fighter for the German air force, proposed a key modification. A cam would be attached to the crankshaft of the engine in line with each propeller blade, and, when the blade reached a position in which it might be struck by bullets from the machine-gun, the relevant cam would actuate a pushrod that, by means of a series of linkages, prevented the gun from firing. Once the blade was clear, the linkages retracted, allowing the gun to fire. This synchronized machine-gun was fitted to the new Fokker E aircraft, which began arriving on the Western Front in late 1915, and gave the German pilots a devastating advantage since, for the first time in the air, the pilot was wedded to his machine; his gun coincided with his eye.

Commissioned by a British publisher, Le Corbusier's *Aircraft* (1935) was the culmination of the architect's obsessive aestheticization of the flying machine over the previous twenty years. Written, he claims, 'to inform the general public, questions of technique apart, as to what stimulus there may be in [the aeroplane] for contemporary society, divided at the moment between a desire to retrace its steps and to embark on the conquest of a new civilization', the book is by turns maddening, stimulating and, in certain respects, disturbing: 'What an unexpected gift to be able to come from above with a machine gun at the beak's tip spitting death fanwise on men crouched in holes'.[9]

Max Ernst, having served in the trenches as an infantryman, certainly knew the experience of being strafed from above, and *Murdering Aeroplane*, one of his early Dada collages, recalls the feeling of being under fire. Circling above the flat horizon, the pulverized landscape of northern France, an aircraft has assumed a monstrous form, half man, half machine. The nose, wing, fuselage

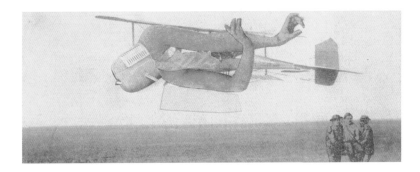

and *empannage* at the tail are constructed out of metal, as expected; but from the forward cowling there emerges a tangle of anatomically impossible arms, the left hand having perhaps just dropped its load over the trio on the blasted land, and the right, with its wrist cocked back, about to fire another dart at the poor bloody infantry. But then we notice that each of the three figures walking out of the frame has one arm either missing or maimed, and the ghastly possibility emerges: this is not a representation of ordinance at all, but rather of spoil, for instead of being dropped as bombs the limbs are now propelled away by the rapacious, silver-beaked machine.

Of course, it may be that Ernst's intention in this rough and ready collage was to imply the technological metamorphosis that took place between 1914 and 1918: the sense that aircraft, once the preserve of eccentric amateurs, were in the hands of a war machine becoming increasingly inhumane. Le Corbusier's account is explicit about the role played by the Great War in the development of aircraft:

> The war was a tremendous lever for aviation. In a feverishly accelerated rhythm, at the command of the State, the order of Authority, all doors were opened to discovery. Success was achieved, the aim reached,

Max Ernst, *Murdering Aeroplane* (1920).

astounding progress made. All this was to kill and destroy . . . If the war had not happened, aviation would still be pottering in poor little workshops of mechanics, in the fields of Lucerne . . . War was the hellish laboratory in which aviation became adult and was shaped to flawless perfection.[10]

The suggestion emerges that as aircraft develop they create a special breed of humanity, 'aces', characterized by their 'reckless courage, foolhardiness, contempt for death'; a breed whose great exploits – flying across the water, over the desert, against the odds – exist in inverse proportion to the fragile contingencies of their machines.

Charles Lindbergh is offered as an example of such an 'ace', a military man, who on Friday 20 May 1927, at 7.52 a.m., took off in a silver-winged monoplane and flew from the United States to France, the 92nd person to fly the Atlantic but the first to fly it alone. His aircraft was a Ryan NYP, based on its M-1, but customized with a massive 237 hp Wright J-5C Whirlwind engine. The wings were specially extended for greater range, but to fly 7,500

Charles Lindbergh's *Spirit of St Louis* takes off from Roosevelt Field, New York, on 20 May 1927, with Paris still 33 hours away.

km (4,650 miles), with a safety margin, demanded 2,700 lb of fuel and meant placing a huge tank in front of the cockpit, blocking all forward vision except by periscope and side windows. For the duration of the 33-hour flight, Lindbergh was effectively flying blind; his machine led the way. Le Corbusier recalled: 'Over night at Paris, the wires announced that Lindbergh was flying over French soil, that at a given hour, in the darkness he would be at Le Bourget. Paris hastens by all roads towards this wonder man. What an ovation. What joy.'[11] Harry Crosby, an American writer then living in Paris, witnessed the landing and described it in his diary:

> Then sharp swift in the gold glare of the searchlights a small white hawk of a plane swoops hawk-like down and across the field – C'est lui Lindberg, LINDBERG! [sic] and there is pandemonium wild animals let loose and stampede towards the plane and C and I hanging on to each other running and the crowd behind stampeding like buffalo and a pushing and a shoving and where is he where is Lindberg where is he and the extraordinary impression I had of hands thousands of hands weaving like maggots over the silver wings of the Spirit of Saint-Louis and it seems as if all hands in the world are touching or trying to touch the new Christ and that the new Cross is the Plane and knives slash at the fuselage hands multiply hands everywhere scratching tearing it.[12]

It seemed that the little Ryan machine, rather than its pilot, was exciting the mass frenzy; a will to consume the machine. Newspaper accounts bore witness to Lindbergh's reaction to the welling crowds: he screamed at the *gendarmerie*, 'For God's sake, save my machine.'[13] Later, his pilot's log barely stated the facts: 'Roosevelt Field, Long Island, New York, to Le Bourget Aerodrome, Paris, France. 33 hrs. 30 min. (Fuselage fabric badly torn by souvenir hunters.)'[14] In his later accounts of the flight, Lindbergh was modest about his own achievement and stressed it was the air-craft that had borne him across the water, and in particular its engineering. In Paris, a few days after he landed, he told news-papermen, 'You fellows have not said enough about that wonderful motor'; and so when Lindbergh returned to Washington and Calvin Coolidge pinned the Distinguished Flying Cross on him, he ensured that proper due was also given to the Ryan. 'For we are proud', said the President, 'that in every particular this silent partner repre-sented American genius and industry. I am told that more than 100 separate companies furnished materials, parts or service in its construction.'[15] Hence, the flight was not the heroic lone success of a single daring individual, but the climax of the co-operative effort of an elaborately connected set of technologies.

A couple of years after the flight, Brecht wrote his cantata *Der Flug des Lindberghs*. His Lindbergh, however, is no hero; at his arrival, he asks to be carried to a dark shed, so that 'no-one sees / my natural weakness'. His flight was sustained for the good of those who built *The Spirit of St Louis*:

Seven men built my machine in San Diego
Often twenty-four hours without a break
Using a few metres of steel tubing,
What they have made must do for me
They have done their work, I
Carry on with mine, I am not alone, there are
Eight of us flying here.[16]

On landing, his mind turns again to those engineers of flight: 'tell my comrades in the Ryan works at San Diego / that their work was good / Our engine held out / their work has no flaws.' Brecht was suggesting that by now the rampant individualism inherent in the early days of powered flight was waning; rather than empowering the flyer, aircraft were superseding the individual. It was a technological narrative even the strongest personality could not resist.

In 1926, the year before Lindbergh's flight, Antoine de Saint-Exupéry landed a job with the company that would become Aéropostale, flying the mail first from Toulouse to Alicante, then extending the route south to Casablanca, Dakar, and on by the shortest route across the Atlantic to South America. It was the making of his reputation as a flier, and a writer, too; and yet it is remarkable how little he seems to have been interested in the technical details of the aircraft he piloted, and crashed; indeed, a recent biographer called him 'the world's greatest Luddite aviator'.[17] Even when Saint-Exupéry devotes a chapter of *Terre des hommes* to aircraft, they remain abstract and unidentified, a means to an end in fact; the flight of the self:

> The more perfect machines become, the more they are invisible behind their function . . . Once we were in contact with a complex workshop. Today we forget the revolving of the engine. It is at last fulfilling its function, which is to revolve just as a heart goes on beating, and we pay no attention to out heart. The tool no longer absorbs out attention.[18]

In 1943, to escape a grim exile in New York, Saint-Exupéry managed to get back into active service with a French squadron, under the command of the USAF, flying Lockheed P-38s. At that time, the machine more commonly known as the Lightning was the fastest fighter in service and had the widest operational range. Twelve metres (38 feet) long, with a wingspan of 17 metres (52 feet), the Lightning was powered by two Allison V17 twelve-cylinder water-cooled engines, each developing 1,475 hp, allowing it to fly faster and higher than most enemy aircraft.

Furthermore, it was the only fighter to be fitted with five weapons – four 12 mm Browning M2 machine-guns and a 20 mm AN-M2 cannon – mounted together in the nose, which lent it great accuracy. The Germans called it the 'Fork-Tailed Devil', the Japanese 'Two Aircraft with One Pilot'; for the poet Gregory Corso it was one of 'the doves of war'.[19]

More than 10,000 were built, but the machines given to the French were barely serviceable; 'war-weary, non-airworthy craft', and for a flyer like Saint-Exupéry, used to flying instinctively, they were a handful, far more complex than the machines with which he had made his name. To his dismay, there were more than 200 dials and controls to monitor; the two engines were linked to six different fuel tanks and, to provide emergency speed, the engines were fitted with a supercharger boost, which would haul the large aircraft to 725 km/h (450 mph). By then his girth was thickening, and he

The Lockheed P-38 Lightning was an advanced design for its time, with a full-vision canopy, tricycle landing gear, turbo-superchargers and formidable armament.

was so crocked by his numerous injuries that he could barely make it into the cramped cockpit. To make matters even more uncomfortable, his plane's heating system was inoperative, and he found the complexities of the flight control system hard to divine: in August 1943 he wrote off a P-38 when he forgot to prime the braking system prior to landing on a short airstrip. Shortly after this accident, he wrote, but never sent, a letter: 'I have just made several flights on a P-38. It's a lovely machine. I would have been happy to have had such a present for my twentieth birthday'; but as the letter continues, however, he turns on the Lightning:

> If I am killed in action, I could not care less. Or if I succumb to a fit of rage over these flying torpedoes which no longer bear any relation to flying and which turn the pilot amid his dials and his buttons into a kind of chief accountant . . . But if I come out alive from this 'necessary and

Antoine de Saint-Exupéry, in the cockpit of his Lightning, 1943.

thankless job', there will only be one question so far as I'm concerned: what can one, what must one say to men.[20]

He knew, as did so many of his comrades, that now the voice of the individual could barely be heard over the roar of the Lightning's propellers, the wail of the War machine.

Uncouth Arts

In 1949 the reclusive British millionaire Henry Kremer, 'a small alert figure, painfully shy', who having made his fortune from fibreglass and plastics now maintained a 'single-minded concern for developing new materials', offered a prize in his own name to be awarded for the first human-powered aircraft to fly a figure of eight course around two pylons half a mile apart; the tight figure of eight circuit offered an infinitely difficult challenge.[21] The prize was originally set at £5,000 and confined to British machines, but as the years passed numerous attempts were made, but with no winners. In 1969 Kremer doubled the prize and opened it to entries from the 'rest of the World'; within eight years, the purse had reached £50,000.

On 23 August 1977, as the early morning sun climbed over Shafter Airport, California, a flimsy transparent structure weighing only 35 kg (70 lb) was gently placed on the runway. Designed by Paul MacCready, a Californian glider expert, the Condor was constructed from thin aluminium tubes covered with Mylar, a thin plastic film made by Dupont, and braced with stainless steel wires. The propeller sat at the back of the plane and was balanced by a stabilizer carried on a long boom at the front; the leading edges of the wings were made of corrugated cardboard and styrene foam. Its pilot, Bryan Allen, a professional cyclist and hang-glider enthusiast, sat semi-reclined, with both hands free: one hand held a handle that controlled both vertical and lateral movement, the other manipulated a lever located beside the seat that controlled wires to twist the wing for turns.

MacCready had only conceived the idea of designing a human-powered aircraft in the summer of 1976. After building several models to test the structure, he and his team began constructing the first complete aircraft in October, the first proving flight, which lasted 40 seconds, taking place on Boxing Day. Throughout the first part of 1977 modifications steadily improved control and efficiency; now, on this late summer day, Allen took to the air at 7.30 a.m. and landed 7 minutes 27 seconds later, having covered the official circuit of 1,850 m (1.15 miles), at a flight speed between 10 and 11 mph. At full flight, Allen's pedalling developed one-third of a horsepower. Two years later the same team created the Gossamer Albatross, another contraption with a similar weight and wingspan, this time to meet the Kremer prize committee's challenge for the first human-powered flight across the English Channel. That flight took almost three hours and covered more than 32 km (20 miles), winning the new prize of £100,000, at the time the largest in aviation history.

Human-powered flight has its origins in a myth about wanting to return home over the water; an escape into nostalgia. The great inventor Daedalus, having created a labyrinth in which to imprison the Cretan Minotaur, given Ariadne the thread to find her way through it, and executed for Pasiphaë the notorious wooden cow is, in a sixteenth-century translation of Ovid's *Metamorphoses*, 'now tired of liuing like a banisht man and prisoner and longs in his heart to see his natiue Clime'. To flee from the island, he turns his mind to secret projects:

to vncoth Arts he bent the force of all his wits
To alter natures course by craft. And orderly he knits
A rowe of fethers one by one, beginning with the short,
And ouermatching still eche quill with one of longer sort
... Then fastned he with Flax
The middle quilles, and ioyned in the lowest sort with Wax.
And when he thus had finisht them, a little he them bent
In compasse, that the verie Birdes they full might represent.[22]

Icarus, of course, ignores his father's precise instruction to keep close to the surface of the sea, and his flying too close to the sun melts the glue holding his wings together. He comes unstuck over the Aegean.

The Gossamer Albatross under test, 1980.

Begun at MIT in the mid-1980s, 'Project Daedalus' was perhaps an attempt to react against some of the more outlandish precepts of the Gossamer aircraft; in particular, the fact that in August 1980 MacCready's team used the radiation that melted Icarus' wings to fuel more than 16,000 solar cells in the wing fabric of a bizarre-looking scaled-down version of the Albatross, and so cause a 3 hp engine to turn a 7 foot propeller. The plane, bizarrely named Penguin, and piloted by a featherweight pilot, Janice Brown, managed to fly two miles across Edwards Air Force Base, California, before landing on the desert floor. The goal of 'Project Daedalus' was quite simply to break, in an entertainingly public manner, the endurance record for human-powered flight, by taking off from Crete and heading to Santorini, 118 km (72 miles) away over the water. The flight was flawless until the pilot, Steve Bussolari, began to tire. As he approached the shore and turned into the northern wind, the ground speed began to drop until the aircraft was almost stationary; after an agonizing holding pattern, Daedalus crashed into the beach, in turn splintering the graphite in the tail boom and ultimately breaking the wing.

This machine, the design of Mark Drela, a young professor of aeronautics, also made use of Mylar to cover the internal structures, but its frame, compounded from Kevlar, a material created for the moon landings, was more recognizably that of a conventional, but very light, aircraft. The fuselage pod was suspended beneath a 8.8 m (29 ft) boom, which supported an 3.35 m (11 ft) propeller turning at about 105 revolutions per minute. Each turn of the pedals was translated by gearboxes into one and a half revolutions of the propeller, and a bell crank enabled Bussolari to adjust the propeller's pitch during flight: low pitch for power on take-off, high pitch for endurance during cruise. He manoeuvred the rudder and elevator with a small control stick in his right hand. Except for a few metal screws, everything in the airplane was handcrafted and meticulously measured, even the 31 kg (68.5 lb) of glue that held together much of the machine of was weighed.

In order to achieve their goals, these designers made use of advanced weight-saving composites, and sophisticated aerodynamic modelling techniques. Yet at the heart of each of the machines was an older, less unfamiliar technology: the bicycle. Seven years prior to the Wright brothers' first flight in December 1903, James Howard Means argued in an editorial for the *Aeronautical Annual* that the bicycle and the flying machine were inevitably connected: 'To learn to wheel one must learn to balance. To learn to fly one must learn to balance.' Even then it was recognized that bicycles and aircraft would have an inherent instability in common, and might share technologies. In August 1896 Otto Lilienthal, the German gliding pioneer who would die a few days later of head injuries sustained testing a rudder modification to one of his devices, wrote a letter to Means to congratulate him on this insight: 'I think that your consideration on the development between the flying machine and the bicycle . . . is excellent . . . I am sure the flying apparatus will have a similar development.' Most remarkable, perhaps, was the perspicacity of the editor of the *Binghamton Republican* who had predicted in June 1896 that the invention of a successful airplane might well be the work of bicycle makers. 'The flying machine will not be in the same shape, or at all in the style of the numerous kinds of cycles, but the study to produce a light, swift machine is likely to lead to an evolution in which wings will play a conspicuous part.'[23]

At this time, in Dayton, Ohio, the Wright brothers – their very surname implying some kind of craft – were living among hollow metal tubes, spoked wheels, chain drives and whatever else it required to construct efficient velocipedes that weighed and cost as little as possible. They also happened to be moved by flight. When they first expressed formal interest in flight by writing to the Smithsonian Institution in 1899 for a reading list on aeronautics, their business was robust. By way of reply, the brothers received a brief bibliography, the contents of which – books and pamphlets then available, including the works of Lilienthal, whose glider designs had made over 4,000 successful flights, L. P. Mouillard, S. P. Langley and Octave Chanute – they sought out and studied. In due course they contacted Chanute, a Chicago-based civil engineer and aeronautical authority, whose book *Progress in Flying Machines* (1894) had become the standard work in the field of aeronautics. Their correspondence would lead to a significant personal and technical relationship between the two brothers and the then famous engineer and inventor.

The Wrights' first ambition was to build a man-carrying kite. After consulting Chanute, and the US Weather Bureau for a suitable location, they settled on a sand bar between Albemarle Sound and the Atlantic Ocean at Kitty Hawk, North Carolina, where stiff sea breezes and soft sand dunes combined to offer perfect conditions for experiments; where Kill Devil Hills, more than 30 metres (100 ft) high with a ten-degree slope, proved ideal as a test range; and where the mosquitoes and the ticks bit them hard. The brothers built their first glider and took it down to Kitty Hawk in the autumn of 1900, where they flew it like a kite controlled by two ropes. Built on the basis of data obtained from the writings of Lilienthal and Chanute, this glider flew on a rope with a 23 kg (50 lb) payload of chains. Encouraged by these efforts, the Wrights returned to Dayton, keen to build a larger glider, which would be flown at Kitty Hawk in the presence of Chanute in late 1901; this, however, proved an embarrassing failure. It was during these trials that the Wrights became convinced that the works of Chanute and Lilienthal contained fundamental flaws, and so they embarked on their own basic experimentation on the optimum shape of aerofoils.

During the winter of 1902–3 they built, in their bicycle shop, a crude wind tunnel; it was fashioned from an old soapbox. From this, they obtained their first experimental confirmation that the data they had been relying on was incorrect. Galvanized, they built a large and more efficient wind tunnel with its airstream propelled by a single-cylinder petrol engine, and now experimented with some two hundred wing shapes. At this point they felt confident in the design of a new glider that would depart radically from earlier technologies of stability and control. This device made more than a thousand flights, far surpassing the previous achievements of Chanute and Lilienthal. Satisifed with their own data, they now determined to build a powered glider; for the remainder of 1903 the bicycle business would be neglected.

The biggest problem still remaining was the means of propulsion. Having designed and built an engine for their wind tunnel, with the help of the mechanic Charles Taylor they now designed and built a lightweight motor that embodied such advanced engineering as direct fuel injection into the cylinders, the use of aluminium, and water cooling. It weighed only 77 kg (170 lb) and delivered between 12 and 16 hp. In developing a propulsion mechanism, the brothers relied on wind tunnels and books on marine engineering; drawing on their earlier bicycle fabrications, they bodged together a crude chain drive to carry power from the engine to the two counter-rotating propellers at the rear of the machine, one chain being crossed to give better rotation.[24]

Having spent much of the autumn at Kitty Hawk tweaking the machine, and waiting for ideal conditions, on the morning of 17 December 1903 Orville took the controls and made four flights,

the longest of 59 seconds and covering 259 m (850 ft). In due course, the poetry of their flight emerged:

> O sinewy silver biplane, nudging the wind's withers!
> There, from Kill Devils [sic] Hills at Kitty Hawk
> Two brothers in their twinship left the dune;
> Warping the gale, the Wright windwrestlers veered
> Capeward, then blading the wind's flank, banked and spun
> What ciphers risen from prophetic script,
> What marathons new-set between the stars![25]

Hart Crane's lines are strangely duplicitous as they draw attention to the strangely recurrent aspect of the two brothers' achievement, and of their 'twinship': their close relationship, naturally, is at issue, as well as the dual structure of their amazing machine, the Wright Flier, a bi-plane, derived, predictably enough, from the bi-cycle.

The moment of flight, Kill Devil Hills, 17 December 1903.

The earliest flight was in one direction only, but in Crane's account the brothers 'banked and spun', perhaps implying that the impetus driving the venture was financial as much as technological. A recent critic has put it neutrally: 'the pioneering voyage has a commercial *raison d'être*, which does not invalidate the pilots' heroism, but objectifies it, and so demonstrates how the lone hero must interact with the impersonal forces of society'.[26] But for the Wright brothers the social interaction became increasingly rare:

> As the flights got longer,
> the Wright brothers got backers,
> engaged in lawsuits,
> lay in their beds at night sleepless with the whine of phantom
> millions, worse than the mosquitoes at Kitty Hawk.[27]

Though they continued to make flights in the two years following the triumph at Kill Devil Hills, they did so with as little publicity as possible; by late 1905, with the patents still pending, the elder brother, Wilbur, was increasingly anxious that their aircraft might be easily copied if it were seen in public at all. Consequently, for almost three years, until May 1908, the Wrights neither flew their machines nor permitted strangers to view them. Geoffrey de Havilland recalled that, in the years following it, their 'epoch-making first flight was almost secret':

> The world heard little about the early exploits of the Wright Brothers, but by 1906 or 1907 word began to filter through to people who were interested in such things that men like Santos-Dumont, Blériot, Voisin, Pelterie and Farman in France, and Cody, Roe and Dunne in England, were meeting with success and were actually making short hops.[28]

These hops would soon lengthen into great leaps forward; in 1909 Blériot, so single-mindedly, would fly across the Channel in a mono-plane: the Wrights' secrecy forced interested parties to develop alter-native designs, often more sophisticated than their own. While the European public was impressed when it finally saw the Wright Flier at Le Mans in August 1908, many of the designers de Havilland men-tions were already looking beyond its configuration, since, despite the 'extraordinary thrilling beauty' of the machine Henry James saw, its technologies – rail-launched, propellers driven by sprocket and chain, forward elevators, wing warping and unpredictable flight characteristics – were resolutely of the nineteenth century. This is the nub: the Wright Flier, the first powered aircraft, looks nothing like the aircraft that were to follow it, yet they in turn do recall the designs of earlier objects that barely left the drawing board.

Flying Objects

In late April 1843 *The Times* carried a report, originating in the *Glasgow Constitutional*, concerning a flight made by Professor Geolls, 'a foreigner', in a hitherto unidentified flying machine. Having described the preparation, take-off and early part of the flight from 'Dumbuck' hill, the correspondent coolly reported that, while over the Ayrshire coast, three steam pipes simultaneously fractured, causing the craft to lose power suddenly and plunge into the water, where the shaken Professor was rescued by a passing steamer.

For once the editors of *The Times* had been taken in by a hoax, one typical of the many circulating at the time intended to ridicule the 'dumb buck' William Henson, a Somerset lace-maker, whose design for the 'Aeriel' was, nevertheless, the prototype of a modern aeroplane.[29]

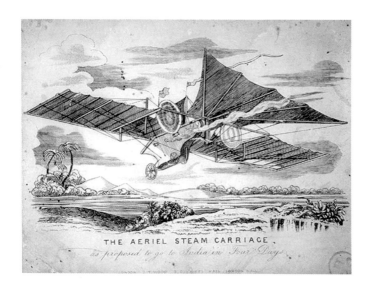

THE AERIEL STEAM CARRIAGE,
as proposed to go to India in Four Days.

The previous year Henson's ambitions for what was later styled the 'Aeriel Steamer' or the 'Aeriel Steam Carriage' had materialized in patent No. 9,478, for which provisional protection was granted. A complete specification with drawings was filed on 28 March 1843, under the title of 'Locomotive Apparatus for Air, Land and Water', and referring in particular to 'Certain Improvements in Locomotive Apparatus and Machinery for conveying Letters, Goods and Passengers from Place to Place through the Air, etc.' He proceeded to describe the contraption as

> an apparatus so constructed as to offer a very extended surface or plane of a light yet strong construction, which will have the same relation to the general machine which the extended wings of a bird have to the body when a bird is skimming in the air; but in place of the movement or power for onward progress being obtained by movement of the extended surface or plane, as is the case with the wings of birds, I apply

A contemporary engraving of William Henson's 'Aeriel Steam Carriage' (1843).

suitable paddle wheels or other proper mechanical propellers worked by a steam or other sufficiently light engine.

He envisaged a huge monoplane, the large rectangular wings of which, spanning some 45 m (150 ft), were not flat surfaces but instead were curved on the tops and undersides, and formed by wooden ribs attached to spars – hollow cylinders that gradually tapered to the ends – and then covered with fabric. Braced with wires, internally and externally, these wings carried two contra-rotating six-bladed propellers, driven by a compact steam engine capable of delivering 25 to 30 horsepower. The machine would weigh 3,000 pounds and for every half pound of weight would have one square foot of surface – a wing surface of 4,500 square feet, a horizontal tail surface of 1,500 square feet. Henson's flight control system worked by means of a web-shaped slab tail-plane and a pilot-controlled vertical rudder. The landing gear was fixed in a tricycle arrangement beneath the cabin, which was slung directly under the wing.

In order to get this machine off the ground, however, funding was required; and the first stage was the creation of a limited company. Henson, along with John Stringfellow, an engineer specializing in weaving machines, Frederick Marriott, then resident at Chard, who would become a well-known journalist in California and would build his own dirigible, the Avitor, and a lawyer, D. E. Colombine, formed a partnership to secure the patent and to construct the machine. The involvement of J. A. Roebuck, then MP for Bath and who sponsored the company's necessary incorporation under an Act of Parliament, served to attract some attention in the press. But Colombine, although responsible for the legal work connected with the patent, was also an experienced publicist, and he commissioned and circulated many illustrations of the proposed machine – now coming to resemble a flying wheelbarrow – in flight over London, the Channel, the coast of France, the Pyramids and China. A pamphlet appeared, entitled *The Full Particulars of the Aeriel Steam Carriage which is intended to convey Passengers, Troops and Government Despatches to China and India, in a Few Days*, containing most of the information that served as the basis for contemporary newspaper articles and proclaiming that the machine, 'the result of years of labour and study, presents a wonderful instance of the adaptation of laws long since proved to the scientific world combined with established principles so judiciously and carefully arranged, as to produce a discovery perfect in all its parts and alike in harmony with the laws of Nature and of science'. Not surprisingly, faced with such vaunting claims, the press became hostile and, despite the construction of several models that Henson vainly attempted to make fly, the project foundered shortly afterwards and he emigrated to New Jersey.[30]

Yet the main features of his design were to be found incorporated, in one way or another, in the majority of aircraft during the early years of successful flight. However bizarrely, Henson assimilated nearly all the available knowledge of his time and applied it most ingeniously in the design of the 'first aeroplane project'. Of course, his approach was not by way of practical full-scale experiments with gliding machines or wind-tunnels – the method by which the Wrights ultimately achieved their flight. Had funds emerged, Henson would apparently have been content to construct a machine from the drawing board, and then provide it with the propulsive power that was known to be essential. Fifty years on, another procedure applied: it was of little use to apply power until an airframe had been built that could be piloted in the air. The irony is that a flying machine that never left the drawing board was more influential, in terms of the 'look' and 'form' of later aircraft, than the Wrights' successful design. Indeed, as competitors to the brothers struggled to get their machines airborne, alternatives were being taken seriously whose provenance was far more fictional than Henson's grand project.

'The future is for the flying machine', proclaimed Santos-Dumont, who in 1906 had become the first man in Europe to fly in a powered aircraft. He was alluding to the pronouncement made by the great inventor hero of Jules Verne's novel *Robur Le Conquérant* (1886), a work which, the Brazilian aviator often claimed, had first caused him to devote his life to aeronautics.[31] Early in the book Verne provides a brief history of nineteenth-century flying machines, consisting of 'some with wings or screws, others with inclined planes, imagined, created, constructed, perfected', but each 'ready to do their work, once there came to be applied to thereby some inventor a motor of adequate power and excessive lightness'. Included in the list, of course, is 'the Englishman Henson, with his system of inclined planes and screws worked by steam'; without his and all the other attempts and experiments of his predecessors, it is clear that Robur could not have conceived 'so perfect an apparatus' as the *Albatross*, an *aeronef* or heavier than air machine. As the novel begins this has made a series of mysterious appearances, leading to reports of aerial trumpets in the heavens and flashes of light in the night sky over Europe and America.[32]

The *Albatross* is constructed on a platform a hundred feet long and twelve feet wide; a ship's deck in fact, with a projecting prow, so that at first glance it might indeed have been called 'a clipper with thirty-seven masts': hence, the English translation as *The Clipper of the Clouds*. Distributed along its deck are thirty-seven vertical shafts (fifteen along each side, and seven, more elevated, in the centre), each bearing two propellers, not very large in diameter, but rotating at tremendous speed. In front and behind are

An engraving of the 'Albatross' from the 1895 edition of Jules Verne's *Robur le Conquerant* (1886).

another two propellers, each with four blades, and of much larger diameter than the verticals; all of the shafts were powered by the still mysterious force of electricity. As young men, Geoffrey de Havilland and his brother were also inspired by this visionary design: 'in our enthusiasm we made numerous drawings and got as far as writing to the makers of electric fans to ask about the thrust and horsepower required'.[33] Perhaps most extraordinary of all was the state of the technology used to create the framework and hull of the *Albatross*, since it seems that 'unsized paper, with the sheets impregnated with dextrin and starch and squeezed in hydraulic presses, will form a material as hard as steel', but one which, at the same time, is light and incombustible, qualities 'not to be despised in an apparatus flying at great heights'. Of course, this design for a paper flying machine exists in the farthest realms of possibility; that is, only on paper. Verne was aware of this since, although he had checked the viability of the design with his engineer friend Badoureau, he told his publisher, 'between you and me, I advise you never to get in a machine like this one'.[34] Indeed, the chapter that sets out the technical aspects of the *Albatross* is subtitled 'One that engineers, designers and other scientists would do well to skip'. And yet, rather than ignoring it, fliers and designers drew on, or at least coincided with some its inspiring technological suggestions. Boeing, for instance, developing the 747 in the late 1960s, and needing to shed as much weight as possible from the original design, turned to Nomex, a highly flameproof chemically impregnated paper (once again developed by Dupont, the company involved in the Gossamer aircraft), which until then had been used only for internal structures. As in Robur's *Albatross*, the material was used externally; all the fairings, where the massive wing joins the fuselage, were formed from specially treated paper.

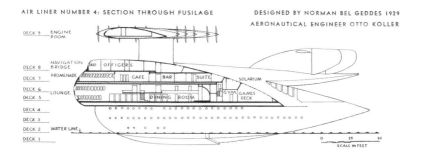

It seems that any design, however unlikely, was worthy of consideration and investigation; before Boeing's engineers began to work on 'the big plane exercise'– the project that would lead to the 747 – their required reading was *Horizons* (1932), Norman Bel Geddes's collection of futuristic transport designs. In it he claimed that, for a number of years, he had been working on plans for a big plane: 'not "big" for the sake of being big', neither 'mad or foolish', but 'sound in every particular', the very idea of the intercontinental airliner of 1940.[35] With the assistance of the German aeronautical engineer Otto Koller, designer of the Pfalz aircraft, so effective in the circuses flying over the trenches fifteen years earlier, he proposed Air Liner Number 4, a tailless, V-winged flying-boat, capable of carrying a total of 606 persons (451 passengers and a crew of 155). It would have had a total wingspan of 528 ft, and on the water would have been supported by two massive pontoons 104 ft apart, 235 ft long and 60 ft high, designed 'substantially as the hull of a yacht, in order to withstand tremendous pounding when the plane rests on a rough sea.' As a means of visual comparison, Bel Geddes suggested that:

> if it were possible to stand her upon one wing tip against the Washington Monument, she would lack only 23 feet of reaching the top.

Cross-section of Air Liner Number 4, designed by Norman Bel Geddes and first published in *Horizons* (1932).

Or imagine that the Public Library was removed from its site in Bryant Park at Forty-second Street and Fifth Avenue, New York. The plane could then settle comfortably in the park with a clearance of about 35 feet all around.

To haul the machine into the air, twenty 1,900 hp motors were to be mounted on an 'auxiliary wing located above the main wing, 180 ft in length by 54 ft in width'. Six extra would be carried as spares, mounted on wheeled carriages: 'by this arrangement it is possible to replace any disabled motor within five minutes. The disabled motor is run over to the machine shop where it can be immediately repaired.'

The plane would have cruised at the stately speed of 100 mph, at a height of only 5,000 feet but with a range of 7,500 miles. The accommodation, spread over nine decks, included 180 apartments, three kitchens, a restaurant for more than 200 people, three private dining-rooms capable of feeding 40 people apiece, an orchestra platform, a dance floor, six shuffleboard courts, a gym, separate solaria for men and women, a library, a writing room and a prom-enade deck. The crew would have included two telephone operators, 24 waiters, seven musicians, two masseuses, a manicurist and a gymnast. Perhaps realizing the questionable airworthiness of certain aspects of his design – not least its gross take-off weight of 570 tons – Bel Geddes states: 'As a premise, one must accept the fact that the air liner I am going to describe will fly, and fly just as readily as any other plane. In fact, I have every reason to believe that it will fly much more smoothly than any plane that has yet been built'. However, to bolster further this wishful thinking, he points out that in the past Koller has developed 'very favourable airfoils for wings and pontoons; streamlines for fuselage; and without exception, all of his planes have flown successfully'.

Despite the precise formulae that Bel Geddes provided in support of his proposed aircraft, there seems to be no absolute form for such designs. Le Corbusier observes, for instance, that 'it would seem "rationally" that the airplane should have a single and unique form. Not at all. There is a differentiation of "harmonies" arising from an individuality which is not to be gainsaid (creation) and resulting in diversified organizations of shape and structure.'[36] Underneath, he prints a photograph of an experimental aircraft designed by the Italian engineer Luigi Stipa, which in appearance resembled a winged dustbin. Perhaps such formal criticism is irrelevant when the only objective is that a given machine should fly freely. Yet the desire to identify style and grace in flying objects is difficult to deny. In the opening moments of *The First of the Few* (1942), Leslie Howard's stirring film account of the life of the Spitfire designer, R. J. Mitchell, it is suggested he was driven only by a desire to create an aircraft that bore no resemblance to the ungainly machines that had been lumbering into the sky

An experimental monoplane with tubular 'venturi' fuselage, conceived by the Italian engineer Luigi Stipa in 1931.

throughout the 1920s; simply, to create an aircraft that could be regarded a piece of functional sculpture. Certainly, its conception is appreciated by 'Rembrandt', one of the real-life RAF pilots featured in the film who, in a lull during the Battle of Britain, admits that he can't 'see a Spit in the air without getting a kick out of it'. As an art student, he is able to appreciate the distinctive line of its wing, and the fact that, although a warplane, it is also an 'artistic job'. Others have suggested that the aircraft's parabolic wing profile is 'as elegant as a Brancusi'; the perfect compromise of its 'small clean fuselage / slim curved wings' making this plane 'British Bauhaus'.[37] Yet the famous wing of the Spitfire, tapered from broad to narrow to distribute stress, was also designed to be just short enough to allow the plane to make tight turns and pull out of steep dives. It was certainly beautiful, but its shape was determined, ultimately, by Mitchell's grasp of aerodynamics, rather than aesthetics.

The converse, of course, is that sometimes technological determinants can render design bizarre rather than beautiful, as in the case of the Blohm und Voss BV 141. In 1937, the year after the Spitfire's first flight, the German Air Ministry (RLM) invited detailed tenders for a new kind of aircraft that would reflect the experiences of the Condor Legion in Spain. These had confirmed the role the Luftwaffe would play in the new strategy of Blitzkrieg: the belief that tank brigades followed closely by motorized troops could make sweeping advances against a conventionally disposed opponent only if that enemy were first pulverized by strategic bombing. The specification, therefore, was a specialist single-engined reconnaissance aircraft with optimum visibility for its crew of three, and which would have a secondary role in supporting army ground units by dropping smoke screens and directing artillery fire.

The Supermarine Spitfire first flew in 1937, and quickly established itself as a masterpiece of aeronautical design.

One of the most serious contenders, the BV 141, was designed by Richard Vogt for Blohm and Voss, a Hamburg-based aircraft company that had been in existence for only five years, a subsidiary of the long-established shipbuilding firm of the same name. Newly appointed, Vogt recognized the challenge and resolved to be daring. In the earliest stages of his research for the commission, it had become clear that conventionally symmetrical airframes might adversely affect the reconnaissance tasks for which the aircraft was intended. His subsequent conjecture was that an asymmetrical craft might perform the role as well as, if not better than, more conservative designs and ensure maximum visibility, both forward (for ground attack) and down (for reconaissance). Hence the aircraft's design was finalized: Vogt placed the crew in a split-level, streamlined pod, shaped like the thorax of a hornet, which projected a

The Blohm and Voss BV141, an asymmetrical prototype designed in 1937.

short distance fore and aft of the wing, but well to the right of the centre line. Just to the left of this glazed cabin, parallel with it, was a long tapering, cylindrical fuselage on which was mounted a radial engine at its front, blending into a conventional tail at the back. At first the Air Ministry officials were sceptical and wary of such an audacious design, but Ernst Udet, the newly appointed head of the Technical Bureau, encouraged Vogt to build a prototype, obliging the Ministry to take a closer look. Once they had flown in it, though, pilots and officials alike were won over by the responsive and forgiving handling of the strange aircraft; Vogt's design theory was vindicated in practice, because having the weight and drag of the cockpit adjacent to the fuselage perfectly countered the torque generated by the single propeller. By January 1940 the Air Ministry was making grandiose production plans. However, the Luftwaffe, its clients, clearly thought the machine

René Magritte, *Le Drapeau Noir* (1937).

too unorthodox in appearance to be taken seriously for a combat role, and it blocked plans for production.[38]

Roughly contemporaneously with the first flights of the Spitfire and the BV 141, René Magritte completed *Le Drapeau Noir* (1937), an oil painting depicting a night sky, cast in grim gunmetallic tones and filled with objects moving in several directions. Later, after the Second World War, Magritte wrote to André Breton and claimed that the painting 'gave a foretaste of the terror of flying machines, and I'm not proud of it'.[39] Perhaps, in retrospect, his decision to figure the aircraft through a variety of domestic objects – coat hangers, hooks, bobbins, candles, shelves and curtained window frames – gives rise to a certain diffuseness, a promiscuity of vision. The title might seem to imply an act of piracy, the raising of a black flag; or even the announcement of the execution of a death sentence. One of the best accounts of the painting suggests that 'it contains the notion of a visitation from another planet worthy of Mack Sennett, but it also brings to mind the eerie hysterical swooping of bats, and the aerial battles of demons in Bosch's *Temptations*'.[40] Yet as well as entertaining such arcane possibilities, the canvas raises a curious technical question: what precisely is it that makes these formal combinations of shapes and objects instantly recognizable as flying machines? Perhaps Magritte was implying the paranoia of a continent whose people, preparing for the inevitable war, saw heavily armed aircraft massing everywhere they looked, and especially when standing anxiously at the windows of their homes. Or is it that the basic shape of aircraft, developed by trial and error over the previous four decades or so, was now so fixed in the public imagination as to be clichéd. It is curious that while the flying objects flagged here are so predictable in their aerial symmetry and connote recognizable machines – monoplanes, biplanes, 'triple-deckers' – the BV 141, although constructed and successfully flown, was unthinkable. In its technologically advanced asymmetry, it looked unnatural; an object that could never fly like a bird, even in one's wildest imaginings.

Framing the Future

In 1923 Hugo Junkers, a German academic turned industrialist who had made his fortune from the invention of a domestic water-heater, was invited to address the Royal Aeronautical Society in London. The most influential aircraft designer of the age, this 63-year-old former Professor of Thermodynamics and Mechanical Engineering at Aachen University – he resigned his post in 1912 – claimed to see in his invitation 'an effort at renewing the ties of a genuine humanity which desires to extinguish the sad traces of devastating war by hoisting the flag of peaceful competition'. The reaction of some distinguished members to his talk, however, was not as constructive as Junkers might have hoped. Frederick Handley-Page, whose firm produced the 0/100, the first British bomber to fly over German positions on the Western Front, took to the floor after the lecture to describe how he had once witnessed the crash landing of a Junkers. The force of the impact caused its fuselage to shear just behind the K painted on its side, so that all he could decipher was the word JUNK – a word which, Handley-Page claimed, encapsulated the Professor's achievements in aeronautical engineering.[41]

Junkers's researches began shortly after the Wrights' European tours of 1908 and 1909 had aroused in this middle-aged man an obsessive interest in the structures of flying machines, to the extent that he added an aviation research centre to his bath water-heater factory at Dessau. Applying the metallurgical expertise he had gained making boilers, and making use of the accidental discovery in 1909 by the German company Durener Metallwerke

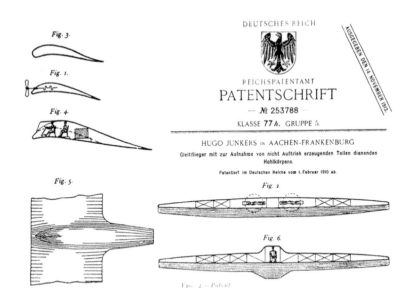

of duralumin, an aluminium alloy containing a little copper and magnesium, Junkers devised a means of constructing aircraft out of such new compounds. Furthermore, in 1910, he patented a design for a flying wing, the Nurflügel; although the extraordinary, modern-looking machine went unbuilt, this patent is the first recorded design of a thick, self-supporting wing. Its basic structural principles led, five years later, to the J.1, a small monoplane powered by a 120 hp Mercedes engine and intended as a scout. This was not simply the first all-metal aircraft, but also featured the first practical cantilevered wing, attached to the fuselage without any of the external bracing wires and struts that typified its competitors, designs against which Leslie Howard's characterization of Mitchell would rail. Its top speed of 170 km/h (105 mph) was agonizingly slow compared with the nervy fabric-covered biplanes of the day, and so it found favour with neither

Hugo Junkers's patent for a flying wing, 1910

pilots nor the German air force, who refused to commission it. Nor did British designers have a better opinion: a machine captured on the Western Front in 1918 was exhibited at to the Agricultural Hall in Islington, London, to the general amusement of the British aeronautical fraternity.

Junkers, however, persevered with his radical designs, now benefiting from the development of more powerful engines, and in 1917 the German Air Service bought his J.4, a two-seat biplane built largely of duralumin, ribbed for added strength, the corrugations running from nose to tail to minimize drag. Though the machine was unwieldy, German airmen liked it for the protection it afforded them. Since it was intended to be a 'trench strafer', and so subjected to heavy small-arms fire, sheet-steel enclosed the cockpits, engine and fuel tank. Before the end of the war Junkers's firm, in collaboration with Fokker, had built nearly 400 military

The four-engine Junkers G38 was the biggest landplane of its time. It had a twin fuselage and seats in the wings giving a unique forward view; a veritable Nurflügel.

aircraft, including two more significant warplanes, the J.9 and J.10, both all-metal cantilevered monoplanes with wings that were attached unconventionally to the underside of the fuselage, and which in the event of a crash landing would hit the ground first, so absorbing some of the impact. After the Armistice, Junkers devoted himself solely to passenger aircraft. A new company, the Junkers-Flugzeugwerke, was established in June 1919 and its first new design, the F.19, a monoplane with an enclosed cabin, and seat-belts for its four passengers, set the standard for post-war air transport. By 1925 Junkers machines had carried about 100,000 people over a total distance of three million miles.[42]

Elsewhere, flight engineering was following an alternative course and an aircraft construction was, in the main, a question of 'a delicate assembly of timber, piano wire, and doped fabric'.[43] Sir Geoffrey de Havilland's first aircraft was typical of the time, but also of the aircraft he would continue to make in the years following the Great War. Airframes were formed out of many components joined together by glueing, pinning or bolting to form a strong but light structure, which was then braced with numerous tensioned wires and the aerodynamic surfaces covered with good fabric such as varnished silk or rubberized, waterproof linen fabric. In 1923 one of de Havilland's machines, the DH.50, was entered for a civil airliner competition at Göteborg, Sweden. Its main rival, flown by Hermann Goering, was the Junkers J.10 monoplane, solidly metal. De Havilland later described his own machine as 'a successful effort to produce a four-seater cabin aircraft at really low cost and upkeep'; in reality it was cheap, flimsy and unpredictable in its handling. Yet the DH.50 won the competition with 999 marks out of a possible 1,000, the company representative identifying his machine's superiority in the fact that there was 'no thin, perishable material whatever in it. Robust wood members and good metal

fishplates throughout. Proved in all climates, and any carpenter can repair it.'[44] Such rough and ready construction would disappear within the decade, to be replaced by an all-metal 'stressed skin' or monocoque structure, in which the metal wrapped around the airframe bears the major part of the structural loads.

Yet the British aircraft industry continued to develop technologies beyond the mainstream. Take the de Havilland Mosquito, developed in the late 1930s as a high-speed unarmed bomber swift enough to avoid interception by even the fast enemy fighter. For various reasons – not least a shortage of metal – it was built of wood by skilled cabinet-makers mobilized from Britain's furniture industry. Its wings were constructed with inner and outer skins of plywood bonded by strong glue to spanwise spruce lengths; the fuselage was made of plywood sandwich with a core of balsa wood, the material often used by aeromodellers. Light alloy and

Junkers Ju-52 under construction, showing the tubular steel airframe which would provide the aircraft with much of its strength.

steel fittings were used as joints at the main stress areas and the airframe was covered by fabric. The aircraft, popularly known as 'The Wooden Wonder', was extraordinarily resilient: flak shrapnel and bullets that would have shattered a metal structure merely holed the timber frame, leaving the machine airworthy. Its losses – only one per 2,000 sorties – were among the lowest in the RAF during the war. A serving pilot wrote a paean to the plane and its makers:

> The Mosquito represents all that is finest in aeronautical design. It is an aeroplane that could only have been conceived in this country, and combines the British genius for building a practical and straightforward

De Havilland Mosquito light bomber, which would enjoy the lowest loss rate of any RAF Bomber Command aircraft during the Second World War

machine with the typical de Havilland flair for producing a first-rate aeroplane that looks right and is right.[45]

The other distinctive construction technique used in the design of certain British bombers was the geodetic form of lattice-work, developed by Barnes Wallis out of his awareness of new developments in airships and hangar building. A 'geodesic' is the shortest line that can be drawn between two points on a curved surface; hence, the massive arched hangars Pier Luigi Nervi constructed for Mussolini's air force in the 1930s depended on a geodetic metal lattice for their strength and durability. Wallis, seeing that an aircraft could be made with equally regular surface curvature all over, developed a metal basketwork in which the entire airframe was assembled from quite small geodetic members pinned together

Piero Luigi Nervi, Aircraft Hangar, 1940, Orbetello, Italy.

at the joints. The first two types of such a design were the Wellesley and Wellington bombers, the latter in particular having such structural integrity that it gained a reputation for bringing crews back from situations that, in conventionally constructed machines, would have seen them dead. Its distinctiveness even emerged into contemporary painting. *Analysis of Easter*, a canvas painted in 1940 by John Armstrong (an associate of Paul Nash, and the costume designer for Sir Alexander Korda's 1936 film, *Things to Come*), seems to imply the resurrective capabilities of such aircraft. Suspended over a pestilent void on thin sticks, and towering above a flower recently sprouted from a broken Easter egg-shell, two flying objects aspire towards gassy clouds. Their wings are tilted up at a curious angle and seem about to commence a synchronized downstroke; but before the image becomes too irrational, the familiar shape to which they are attached comes into focus – the latticed fuselage of the Wellington, which by early 1940 was the mainstay of Bomber Command, and which had given hope to the crews prepared to sacrifice all for the

Vickers's Wellington production line in 1940, showing the geodesic construction of the aircraft's fuselage.

defence of King and Country. In 1980 Prince Charles cited Wallis's geodetic construction as an example of a British technology that had received insufficient recognition abroad.[46] However, though strong, the difficulty of its manufacture, and the fact that it could only ever be covered by fabric, meant that it was of limited value in the new world of aircraft design that emerged from the ruins of Nazi Germany.

'Operation Paperclip', the Allied undertaking to absorb Germany's scientific expertise, took effect the moment the European war was over. As soon as the surrender was signed, teams of British and American experts swooped into Germany, and, picking through the remains of the Reich's war machine, were astonished by what they discovered. De Havilland's design chief, Ronald Bishop

John Armstrong, *Analysis of Easter* (1940).

(responsible for the Mosquito), visited the Messerschmitt plant at Oberammergau, Bavaria, and was stunned at the sophisticated nature of the prototypes he saw: the Me 262, a twin-jet fighter-bomber and by general agreement the finest airframe of the war; the Me 264, a large four-engined, long-range jet bomber, intended to attack America; and Projekt 1007, which Messerschmitt claimed could carry a large load at 885 km/h (550 mph) for almost 7,250 km (4,500 miles), and which would heavily influence Bishop's next design, the ill-fated passenger jet, the Comet. The British engine designer Roy Fedden gloomily reported that 'Germany possessed aeronautical research and test equipment in advance of anything existing in this country or America at the present time'; and representatives of US firms, such as Boeing, were equally amazed at the advanced airframe technology.[47]

George Schairer, the Seattle company's chief aerodynamicist, then working on a jet bomber for the USAF, was assigned to the aeronautical research institute at Braunschweig, where he came across drawings of swept-wing aircraft and wind tunnel data relating to them. He questioned Adolf Büsemann, one of the institute's aerodynamicists, who quickly responded: 'Don't you remember? Rome? Volta Scientific Conference in 1935? You remember my paper on supersonic aerodynamics? . . . No one paid any attention.'[48] In October 1935, Büsemann, a young engineer, had presented a paper on the 'arrow wing', a futuristic concept which argued that if the wings of a plane could be swept back, they might fall within the shockwave cone streaming from the nose of the craft, and so would thus have less drag than straight wings. Although this theory would, within a decade, provide the means by which aircraft could be built to fly faster than sound, Büsemann's calculations attracted little interest at the conference; indeed one of the organizers, General Arturo Crocco, facetiously sketched 'Busemann's aircraft' on the

back of a menu; it had sweptback wings, a sweptback tail and a sweptback propeller to match. But in another part of the future Axis, Germany, Büsemann's theory of airframes would be taken much more seriously. There the Luftwaffe was experimenting eagerly with a number of provocative aircraft designs and his work eventually caught the attention of Woldemar Voigt, the senior designer at Messerschmitt. In 1942 Voigt decided to try out Büsemann's idea in an experimental jet referred to as 'Projekt 1101', the wings of which were to be angled back sharply, in marked contrast to the barely swept wings on the Me 262 he was then developing. Work on Projekt 1101 continued sporadically, with Voigt unable to give it his full attention owing to his involvement with the 262. However, wind-tunnel tests on models of the swept-wing jet were so promising that in 1944 Voigt had commenced development of a research

X-5 experimental 'variable geometry' aircraft.

plane with variable wings that could be repositioned in flight; it was this machine that was captured by the Allies in 1945, and which led to the development of the Bell X-5 experimental aircraft.

Having absorbed much of this advanced research, George Schairer returned from Germany in August 1945 and set out to redesign Boeing's jet bomber as a swept-wing design. By November a radical design had emerged for a machine that would be known, eventually, as the B-47 Stratojet; a silver machine with long razor-thin wings, sweeping back from each side of the fuselage at an angle so sharp that, seen from above or below, it did, indeed, give the profile of an arrowhead; wings under which were slung, in four bullet-shaped pods, six turbojet engines to propel this bomber at 600 mph through the thin air at higher altitude to deliver its atomic weapon at the heart of the enemy. The B-47 would exert as great an influence on future developments in military aviation as any machine since Blériot's monoplane; but its sleek form and sophis-ticated airframe would also lead directly to an aircraft that would alter the world of air transport even more radically.

In mid-May 1954 a large aircraft painted in a sickly livery of yellow and brown was rolled out of a hangar at the Boeing plant in Seattle. The Dash 80 prototype, a swept-wing jet-powered military

The Boeing B-47 Stratojet bomber, the mainstay of the US nuclear strike force by the early 1950s.

transport, and in-flight refueller, was intended to complement the B-47 bomber, the aircraft on which its airframe was largely based. When she launched it, by swinging a champagne bottle at a cage that fractured the glass but stopped it short of the aircraft's delicate aluminium skin, Bertha Boeing, the wife of the founder of the company, exclaimed 'I christen thee airplane of tomorrow.'[49] Within a few months the USAF had ordered a substantial number of the tankers, but the airlines were less than interested in the Dash 80, which they felt was too obviously a by-product of military procurement. The project languished until, pushed by the Pan-Am chairman, Juan Trippe, Boeing's management sanctioned the construction of a revised model, the 707, slightly larger and with more powerful engines that would allow it to fly non-stop across the Atlantic, delivering 120 passengers at a time into the jet age, at the speed of a nuclear bomber.

A Boeing 707-320, in service with Lufthansa in the early 1960s.

2 | Conquests of the Air

Mass Destruction

On 28 August 1940 Bertolt Brecht, marooned in Finland, was updating the journal he had begun a couple of years earlier: a scrapbook of photographs, press cuttings and random observations reflecting the state of his world. As an illustration of what he termed 'the poetry of objects' he pasted a photograph of the cockpit of a Junkers bomber, and wrote nearby: 'the beauty of an aeroplane has something obscene about it'. His entry then recalls that in Sweden before the outbreak of the war, he had suggested making a film on the subject of 'the aeroplane for young workers', a project which would 'give expression to man's basic dream of flying'. His audience was horrified at the idea, and responded shortly: 'you surely don't want them to be bomber pilots?'[1] Now, however, as he wrote, Brecht knew that over the great cities of northern Europe those 'young workers' were indeed sitting at the controls of heavy aircraft, crawling in echelon beneath the cloud-floor, laden with high explosive and incendiary materials, eager to deliver what had been so often promised in the two decades since the Great War ended.

By late August 1940 the Battle for France had been over for several weeks, and that of Britain was well under way. Although

Cockpit of a Junkers 52, as reproduced by Brecht in the pages of his *Journal*, August 1940.

RAF bases had been targeted by the Luftwaffe since the beginning of the month, no German bombs fell on central London until the 24th; and even these, it seems, had been dropped accidentally by a wayward formation. The following day Churchill ordered Bomber Command to attack Berlin in retaliation. The raid had a shocking effect on the German people and their leader, as did fresh bombings of the Reich's capital during the last days of the month. Hitler, incandescent with rage, addressed the German people on 4 September and promised to repay the RAF raids in kind: 'The British drop their bombs indiscriminately on civilian residential communities and farms and villages . . . If they attack our cities, we will rub out their cities from the map.'[2] Three days later, on 7 September 1940, the Blitz would begin.

As an illustration of the concept of the 'The Bird's Eye View' – defined roughly as 'a new function added to our senses . . . a new standard of measurement . . . a new basis of sensation' – Le

A four image spread from Le Corbusier's *Aircraft*, consisting of, moving clockwise from top left: 'La Garde de Guérin en Lozère, France'; 'the Jewish quarter of Tetuan'; 'native huts on the banks of the Chatt-el-Arab'; and Douglas DC-3s over New York, 1935.

Corbusier's *Aircraft* (1935) offers a compelling double-page image sequence.[3] Reading clockwise from the top left are photographs of La Garde de Guérin, an abandoned village in Lozère, '800 m up, with ruined fortifications'; of the Jewish quarter of Tetouan, then a Spanish protectorate in Morocco; and of 'native huts on banks of the Chatt al Arab' river, near Basra in Iraq. Finally, at the end of the sequence, is an image of two large aircraft, shiny new Douglas DC-3 'Dakota' airliners, flying in formation over New York, with the skyscrapers of lower Manhattan clearly visible under their wings. Hence the tour moves through earlier versions of urban plans, before arriving at two key modern phenomena of most interest to

Fritz Lang, *Metropolis* (1926): the City, connected by flying machines.

Le Corbusier in his proclamation of the new age of mechanical civilization: aircraft and the vertical city. This was by no means original: in the previous decade the juxtaposition of these two soaring icons of the modern world – flying machine and sky-scraper – almost proved the ascendancy of the metropolis. Hence, Fritz Lang's visionary film shows aircraft circling like moths beneath the canyon-like walls of factory towers and office blocks. In its own right, each object reinforced the technological advancement; but the conjunction of plane and building led some to greatly fear the direct consequences; a step back, rather than forward. After all, it is easy to see that if the sequence of images described above were read counter-clockwise from the lower left, it would lead only to abandonment and ruin.

In an early short story, 'The Argonauts of the Air', H. G. Wells grimly predicted the future of the flying machine: 'In lives and in treasure the cost of the conquest of the empire of the air may even exceed all that has been spent in man's great conquest of the sea. Certainly it will be costlier than the greatest war that has ever devastated the world.'[4] By 1907 he was prepared to be more specific about these costs; his *The War in the Air* described the destruction by the German Air Fleet – airships – of New York, 'the first of the great cities of the scientific age to suffer the enormous powers and grotesque limitations of aerial warfare'. Watching from his vantage point on the *Vaterland* high above Manhattan, Bert Smallways witnesses the shattering of the world:

As the airships sailed along they smashed up the city as a child will shatter its cities of brick and card. Below, they left ruins and blazing conflagrations and heaped and scattered dead; men, women, and chil-dren mixed together as though they had been no more than Moors, or Zulus, or Chinese. Lower New York was soon a furnace of crimson flames, from which there was no escape. Cars, railways, ferries, all had ceased, and never a light led the way of the distracted fugitives in that dusky confusion but the light of burning.[5]

Even at this stage, Wells realized how, although certainly destructive and demoralizing, air power alone could not occupy territory; only after a city had been razed to the ground could it then be taken. The experience of German air raids during the Great War confirmed his forecasts. In May 1917 a score of Gotha G. IV bombers, massive twin-engined biplanes each capable of carrying 500 kg (1,100 lb) of ordnance, bombed Folkestone, killing 95 civilians. A few weeks later a flight of seventeen Gothas droned over London 'serenely, insolently and practically with impunity' as an Air Vice-Marshal later said, and dropped nearly two tons of bombs in two minutes. One bomb smashed into the Upper North Street School, killing eighteen children and wounding thirty. In all, the German bombers made a dozen raids on England, delivering some 50 tons of bombs. Among the damage noted by newspapers at the time was the flattening of the Odhams publishing house responsible for Horatio Bottomley's rabid anti-German magazine, *John Bull*; the destruction of a wing of the Royal Hospital in Chelsea; and the razing of 23 houses in Maida Vale by a single large bomb. All told, 162 people were killed and 432 were injured, while the Gothas carried out their work untouched by British fighters or flak.

In *The Outline of History* (1920), Wells predicted that future conflict would leave Europe ravaged by air attacks, making the 'bombing of those "prentice days", 1914–1918, look like "child's play".[6] In the early 1920s, enthusiasts for aerial warfare looked forward to conflicts in which high-explosive, incendiary and gas bombs would be used to blast apart factories, burn cities and poison people; in effect, urban populations were to become legitimate military targets. In Britain, Hugh 'Boom' Trenchard, commander of the independent bombing force in the First World War, believed that the first mission of an air force was to defeat the enemy's nation, and that the best form of defence was an attack on the enemy's heartland; he even went so far as to suggest that the effect of bombing on enemy morale would exceed, by a factor of twenty to one, the impact of physical destruction.[7] In 1925 the military historian and theorist B. H. Liddell-Hart confirmed that the enemy's population was the proper object of war, the principal role of air forces being 'to strike the nerve systems of the enemy nation, in which its industrial resources and communications form the Achilles heel'.[8] And, it seemed, nothing could touch the bomber; prior to the development of radar in the late 1930s, few experts believed that either anti-aircraft artillery or fighter planes might ever defeat waves of bombers. Giulio Douhet, whose book *The Command of the Air* was so influential, reasoned that 'Nothing man can do on the surface of the earth can interfere with a plane in flight, moving freely in the third dimension'.[9] Beyond such high-mindedness, his theory had a dark heart: since aircraft were not built for defence, and their only role was being offensive, any distinction that had existed between combatants and civilians could no longer apply. Addressing the House of Commons in November 1932, Prime Minister Stanley Baldwin famously declared:

> I think it well also for the man in the street to realize that there is no power on earth which can protect him from bombing, whatever people tell him. The bomber will always get through . . . The only defence is in offence, which means you have got to kill more women and children quicker than the enemy if you want to save yourselves.[10]

Baldwin's statement and Wells's post-Great War prophecies suggested that modernity had become the helpless victim of the tools that its sciences had perfected. Confronted with the increasing accuracy of new bomb-sighting mechanisms, and the long range of the new heavy bombers, many nations in the 1930s worked frantically to attain comprehensive agreements to disarm air forces, and welcomed the solemn promises of the signatories to the 1928 Kellogg-Briand Pact, which had vainly attempted to outlaw war. Nevertheless, a sense of imminent destruction hung heavy in the air over European cities.[11]

As it proceeds, Le Corbusier's *Aircraft*, too, seems to exhibit a similar sense of urban destruction. After the DC-3 sequence, he presents several more aerial shots, but the message they carry is now delivered as a bombshell in explosive capitals: 'Cities will arise out of their ashes'. His book was subtitled '*L'Avion accuse. . .*', and, as this long section continues, the extent to which Le Corbusier expects flying machines to prosecute their indictments becomes dismayingly clear: 'Cities are old, decayed, frightening, diseased. They are finished.' That last brief sentence seems less a description than a threat, and so there eventually emerges the architect's final solution: 'Cities must be extricated from their misery, come what may. Whole quarters of them must be destroyed and new cities built.' Below this stark imperative, Le Corbusier places an image of a building site – or more likely, a bomb site – above a stark caption: 'Demolition in the Boulevard Haussmann after the War'.[12] The new method for knocking down buildings, it seems, was simple and certain, if a little random. For by this point, however, *Aircraft* is setting down the shape of things to come; a new order, raining down from the sky, clearing the ground for foundations built on scorched earth.

Hence, in his screenplay for Sir Alexander Korda's film *Things to Come* (1936), a necessary compression of his massive history of

the twenty-first century, *The Shape of Things to Come* (1933), Wells would not only visualize destruction, but also renewal, from the air. In his book's first section, 'Today and Tomorrow: The Age of Frustration Dawns', he describes the decline of European civilization in terms of architecture, echoing Le Corbusier's suggestion that the simplest, indeed the only, route out of economic difficulties lay in the modernization and rebuilding of housing stock, rather than in the erection of air-raid shelters; 'immense, usually ill-built concrete cavern systems'. As it happened, such structures could not prevent the noxious effects of the thousands of gas canisters dropped across Europe by those bombers of the Second World War, a conflict which would break out, Wells predicts, in 1940. It is noted coolly that 'the memoirs of the airmen who did so much

'Demolition in the Boulevard Haussmann after the War', reproduced by Le Corbusier in *Aircraft*.

destruction are amazingly empty . . . they do not seem to have had an inkling of the effect of the bombs they dropped on the living flesh below.' After these attacks, his book envisages a 30-year break in civilization, the terrible vacuum filled by a new barbarism and 'The Raid of the Germs', a global pestilence that follows in the bombers' wake. Only in the early 1970s would a new order emerge, out of southern Iraq; more precisely, from the banks of the Shatt al Arab river, close to Basra, where a group of 'technical revolutionaries', known collectively as the 'Air Dictatorship', sought to create a new world, its progress manifested in 'new cities, new roads, continually renewed houses everywhere', and an aerial police force who travel the world's airways making peace. Flying high over areas of unrest, its aircraft drop bombs containing the new gas 'Pacificin', a nerve agent which rendered victims insensible for 36 hours without any side-effects.[13]

Wells's screenplay makes much of the Basra Bomber, the great machine; it is 'less like an aeroplane than a flying fort' that transports the Airmen around the world and which is, in effect, the engine for the renewal of civilization.[14] When he saw Lang's *Metropolis*, Wells complained about the film's mediocre presentation of future design and technology: 'Where nobody has imagined for them, the authors have simply fallen back on contemporary things. The aeroplanes that wander above the great city show no advance on contemporary types.'[15] By comparison, the Basra Bomber looks like no aircraft yet built: massive, twin-tailed, its great wings the shape of a boomerang, in contrast to a double-deck fuselage so bulbously squat. (It is obvious that several aspects of the machine's design were borrowed from Norman Bel Geddes's air liner.) The crew stand and watch from a great window on the promenade deck as their aircraft is attacked by a swarm of battered Avro 504s, fighters 'out of the ark' whose futile manoeuvres are

commanded by the barbarian chief, the Boss. Spectating from below, he can only wave his fist at the 'clumsy great things' massing over his domain, their sophisticated array of armaments swatting away the squadrons of flimsy biplanes like summer flies. As the great aircraft continue serenely beyond the clouds, they release bombs the size and shape of ostrich eggs, each containing the incapacitating agent now known simply as the 'Gas of Peace'. On contact with the ground the spheres shatter, releasing their contents, which will, through the 'Rule of the Airmen', bring 'a new life for mankind'. For Wells it seemed that the bomber, so long synonymous with random destruction, now had the power to change the world.

Screaming from the Sky

In *The Mint*, T. E. Lawrence (aka 'Aircraftsman Ross') asserts: 'the conquest of the air is the first duty of our generation . . . By our

The Basra Bomber, as featured in *Things to Come* (1936), directed by William Campbell Menzies.

handling of this, the one new big thing, will our time be judged.'[16] In *Seven Pillars of Wisdom*, published a decade or so earlier, he had reported on the effects such aerial triumphalism had on his Arab comrades, when in September 1918 a Handley-Page 0/400 bomber flew over the desert to the Sherifian HQ behind Turkish lines, and swooped down with stores of petrol and spare parts for two Bristol Fighters stranded there. As Lawrence watches the big plane drift onto the desert runway, he 'perceived a single Bedawi, running southward all in a flutter, his grey hair and grey beard flying in the wind, and his shirt . . . puffing out behind him. He altered course to pass near us, and, raising his bony arms, yelled "The biggest aeroplane in the world", before he flapped on into the south to spread his great news among the tents.' Lawrence continues: 'At Um-el-Surab the Handley stood majestic on the grass, with Bristols and [D.H.]9s like fledglings beneath its spread of wings. Round it admired the Arabs, saying, "Indeed and at last, they have sent us THE aeroplane, of which these things were

Stuart Reid, *Deraa* (1918–19), showing Arabs welcoming a Handley-Page bomber.

foals".[17] Such an anecdote was typical of the policy of the time; conquest amounted to teaching the lessons of modern civilization to those cowering beneath the wings of one's aircraft.

Impressed by aerial interventions against the Turks during the later stages of the Great War, and desperate to provide the new air force with a rationale, 'Boom' Trenchard had concentrated a major part of the surviving RAF in North-east Africa and the Middle East, in a wide-ranging campaign of 'colonial policing', a concept originally suggested by Churchill. In Egypt in 1919, while aircraft delivered mail, relieved remote garrisons, patrolled railway lines and dropped proclamations, they were also used to bomb and strafe groups of Bedouin and break up concentrations of people in the Nile Delta. In the opinion of a senior officer in the RAF, 'the lesson taught by the events in Egypt during the last seven weeks clearly indicates the imperative necessity for the permanent maintenance of at least three service squadrons in Egypt, supplemented by one or two long distance squadrons of Handley-Page types.'[18] However, it was the success of the RAF in Iraq that proved to the British authorities that bombers could fulfil a constructive 'political' role; eight RAF squadrons quelled a rebellion that almost forty Army battalions had been unable to control. Confronted with sporadic tribal skirmishing, the squadrons swiftly evolved their rules of engagement, which would remain in place until the next war. After investigating reports of disturbances, aircraft – originally Bristols and Ack 9s, hand-me-downs from the war in France, but later Westland Wapatis and Hawker Hardys, specially developed for the air policing role – would scatter leaflets (and occasionally summonses) in English and Arabic. If these failed to quell dissent, aircraft of the Communications Flight were sent in; large, bulbous Vickers Valentia biplanes had loudspeakers fitted on their undersides through which intentions to attack were declared, a procedure known in the RAF as 'sky-shouting'. Should unrest continue, heavy bombers were dispatched and, in an early manifestation of surgical strikes against Iraqi targets, the pilots were briefed to aim for dwellings of tribal leaders.[19]

Coincidentally perhaps, Le Corbusier's *Aircraft* contains two desert photographs, the first of a native camp, a 'nomad's outpost' in French East Africa, and the second of a filling station for aircraft in the middle of the Sahara, a facility Le Corbusier terms a 'nerve centre on the imperial highway'. Clearly, the intention was to suggest the gulf between the natural creations of desert people and the inhuman constructions of European civilization, a gulf which had become apparent when he had overflown the Algerian desert in 1933 in order to view the landlocked cities of the M'Zab:

> Durafour, steering his little plane, pointed out two specks on the horizon, 'There are the cities! You will see!' Then, like a falcon, he stooped several times upon one of the towns, coming round in a spiral, dived, just clearing the roofs, and went off in a spiral in the other direction; then, high in the air, he started farther off. Thus I was able to discover the principle of the towns of the M'Zab. The airplane had revealed everything to us, and what it had revealed provided a great lesson.[20]

Le Corbusier is grateful for the architectural lesson the aerial view gave him. Below, however, Durafour's repeated swoops and dives were causing panic in the streets: 'The women had dashed under the arches on hearing the noise of the engine. The whole town was under the arcades, watching the airplane make its spiral.' Little wonder that the inhabitants sought shelter; over the preceding decades, in other deserts in Africa and the Middle East, Europe's aircraft had already been used to provide an 'incalculable moral example' of governmental authority to 'uncivilized' and 'primitive'

peoples, in just another version of the 'Rule of the Airmen' seen in Wells's prophetic fiction.

In fact, Le Corbusier was particularly drawn to machines whose existence seemed only to demonstrate the sheer authority of the air. A series of photographs of the Savoia-Marchetti SM 55X flying-boat adorn the book, a beautiful machine inevitably associated with the aerial armadas commanded by Italo Balbo, later to become Mussolini's Air Marshal. In December 1930 Balbo led 12 of these aircraft on a flight of 10,500 km (6,500 miles) from the lagoon at Orbetello to Rio de Janeiro. Then, in the summer of 1933, he guided a fleet of two dozen of these machines to the United States, on a route taking them via Ireland, Iceland, Labrador and Montreal, 23 of them arriving at the World's Fair in Chicago intact, on schedule and in perfect formation. Four days later they flew to New York to great acclaim, before heading out over the Atlantic again, to arrive back in Italy on 12 August. The trip was designed as a commemoration of the first ten years of Mussolini's dictatorship, and announced not simply that Italy was at the forefront of an aviation technology that was reliable and would run on time,

Savoia-Marchetti SM 55X flying-boat, a squadron of which were flown around the world by Balbo's pilots.

but that no city was now invulnerable to a visit from its proven warplanes.[21] Perhaps this potential led Le Corbusier to include the SM 55X so frequently in *Aircraft*, depicting it in flight, at rest, under maintenance and, most strikingly, 'Controlling Manoeuvres', in a photograph which juxtaposes the Savoia-Marchetti's great 700 hp propeller engine with a megaphone brandished by a helmeted airman. Le Corbusier helpfully explains that 'the megaphone "directs" the movements of an Italian squadron', but the image clearly implies that Balbo's machines, having so clearly trumpeted the aeronautical achievements of the Duce's nation, were now just as much tools of ideology and government as the airborne loudspeakers that broadcast their success (along with other starker messages) across the deserts of Libya and Abyssinia.

Le Corbusier's book also included three images of the most extraordinary of all propaganda machines, the 'Maxim Gorki'. This

A photograph of the SM 55X Le Corbusier selected for his book, with the caption: 'Controlling Manoeuvres: the megaphone "directs" the movements of an Italian squadron'.

vast aircraft was built through a public subscription organized by the Union of Soviet Writers and Editors, and was intended as a celebration, through technology, of the 40-year literary career of the great Russian author. In terms of its size, the plane, which first flew in May 1934, was as imposing as the Soviet nation: its wings spanned 80 m (260 ft), 20 m wider than that of the Boeing 747, and along their leading-edges were arrayed six of its eight huge 900 hp engines, the other two mounted as a tractor-and-pusher pair in a pod above the fuselage. In all, its powerplant churned out 7,000 hp. It was the 'Gorki's political facilities, however, that provided its most astonishing feature. The rear fuselage housed a cinema into which the local populations encountered during the plane's frequent refuelling stops on journeys across the remote steppes were invited to watch propaganda films. The interior of the left wing contained a publicity office complete with rotary printing press, while a darkroom was installed in the right. The aircraft's eleven cabins were connected by a sophisticated network of telephones, augmented by a system of pneumatic tubes, to allow the physical transmission of propaganda from room to room. Part of the 'Gorki's rationale was the popularization of the aged writer's works across the great

The Ant 42 'Maxim Gorki', the world's largest land plane, constructed in 1934, and written off the following year.

nation; hence, four auxiliary generators produced sufficient electrical power to drive huge loudspeakers on the underside of the aircraft, through which might emerge passages from *Memories of Lenin*, interspersed with exhortations about the Five-Year Plan. At night, as the plane flew low over remote towns, a system of 80 red lights arranged along the fuselage flashed slogans; 12,000 watts of power in the service of the Party.

In 1935 Saint-Exupéry, a guest of the Soviet Union, was invited aboard the aircraft and taken for a flight, the first foreigner to be given such an honour. Exhausted after his guided tour of the 'Gorki's facilities, he sat in a chintz armchair in one of the forward cabins and gazed out of the window, imagining momentarily that he was sitting on the balcony of a grand hotel, beyond the clouds. Here, he observed, one passed from the realm of the machine into that of leisure, of dream. Just 24 hours later the dream became the nightmare, as the 'Maxim Gorki' crashed while undertaking a propaganda flight over Moscow; it was carrying 36 passengers, employees of the city's Central Aerodynamic Institute, most of whom had worked on the machine. As the 'Gorki' began its final approach, an escort fighter lost control and collided with the top of its wing, becoming lodged between two of the engines. Grievously damaged and engulfed by flames, the aircraft slowly came apart in the air, spewing out bodies and equipment from a height of several thousand feet. All the passengers and crew were killed, along with the eight crew, fighter pilot and three residents of a small house struck by massive pieces of wreckage, falling like bombs. The loss of the aircraft led to a period of international mourning, although the leader article in the *New York Times* was less sympathetic to the construction of further giant aircraft: 'How far is it desirable, and how far is it possible, for this process to go? Clearly it has definite limits. National pride, and the human desire to own or construct the "largest airplane in the world", just because it could be called that, have probably had a great deal to do with the matter.' However, because of his proximity to the disaster, Saint-Exupéry's response was the most distinctive: 'Flying its peaceful route towards this bloody intersection, the 'Maxim Gorki' was struck because it found itself in the way of an unsighted fighter plane moving with the speed and trajectory of a bullet.'[22] The message was simple: a civilian machine had been removed from the sky by a weapon of war.

At the time, however, there was a growing perception that civil aircraft, rather than being supplanted by military machines, were co-terminous with them. For instance, *Aircraft* prints a photograph of three tri-motored Wibault 282s bearing the colours of Air France, and carries the caption: 'The new "diligences". Transport of passengers and goods. The new rails are in the air, straight from one continent to another'; below this, in gloomy

The Fairey Hendon night bomber, its airframe constructed entirely from metal, was brought into service in the early 1930s.

outline, is an image of a Fairey Hendon, described by Le Corbusier as a 'bomb carrying airplane', an example of 'the new artillery whose range is unlimited', and which, alternatively, could 'hold 25 men in lieu of bomb load', ferrying them, like goods, from country to country.[23]

Just over a year after *Aircraft* was published, senior Nazi officials requisitioned a large number of three-engined airliners from the German national airline, Lufthansa. The aircraft, Junkers 52s affectionately known by their crews as *Tante Ju* or 'Auntie Annie', had been in service for a couple of years with several European airlines and had quickly established a reputation for reliability and solidity.[24] Their rugged tubular steel frames and stressed skin monocoques gave amazing structural strength; in fact, constructed as they were out of corrugated duralumin, into which were cut large rectangular windows, they resembled light industrial workshops with wings. The aircraft took off from Tempelhof airport, Berlin, on an 11-hour flight that took them first to Morocco and then to

A Lufthansa Junkers Ju 52 in flight. Renowned for its safety and economy, the tri-engine aircraft, nicknamed *'Tante Ju'*, was put into Lufthansa service in 1933.

Nationalist-controlled Seville. The operation – *Zauberfeuer* – had to begin secretly because Hitler was unwilling to challenge directly states sympathetic to the Republican cause, especially when, at this early stage in the Spanish Civil War, the fate of the Nationalist revolt was uncertain. The journey was an arduous undertaking for the flight crew, requisitioned along with the aircraft. One plane landed in Republican-held territory by mistake, and its members were incarcerated for several days before the German ambassador managed to secure their release by protesting indignantly about the illegal seizure of a commercial aircraft, which was after all the sovereign territory of the Reich. Meanwhile, at the beginning of August 1936, a large number of Luftwaffe pilots left Hamburg aboard the steamer *Usaramo*, travelling incognito as members of an ersatz tour group, the Union Tour Society. The ship's hold had been loaded with 800 crates containing the

A Junkers Ju 52 of the German-Russian DERULUFT airline, founded in November 1921. This photograph was taken in 1935.

components of six Heinkel 51 biplane fighters and ten more Junkers 52s.[25]

By the second week of August, history's first concerted military airlift was proving blazingly successful. The Junkers commandeered from Lufthansa shuttled across the narrows from Morocco to the Spanish mainland, their pilots making as many as five round-trips each day. Crammed into cabins originally designed to hold only seventeen paying passengers would be, on occasions, three dozen or more Moroccan soldiers, drawn from the areas around Tetouan, their tribal robes tucked around their knees. The interior fitting of the Junkers had now been stripped out and, to compound their discomfort, many of the troops, unaccustomed to flight, also became sick in the turbulent air over the straits of Gibraltar. Nevertheless, by early October 13,000 men had been transported to Spain, along with roughly 500 tons of ammunition and other equipment, including 36 howitzers. From the outset the aircraft flew unarmed and with registration markings painted out, but for some of the more fanatical air-crew the temptation to participate in combat was too powerful to resist. On 13 August, after several Junkers 52s drew anti-aircraft fire from a moored Republican cruiser, one flight engineer rigged a weapons bay in the floor of his aircraft – a simple conversion the plane's sturdy airframe was well suited for – and bombed the offending vessel, inflicting damage that kept it out of service for several months.

In the early days of German intervention such exploits were isolated and unauthorized. But once the airlift had concluded in October 1936, Hitler, encouraged by his Air Minister, Goering, chose to take a more active, if still covert, part in the Spanish conflict; after all, the previous months had demonstrated that this compact theatre of war might be a useful proving ground for the

Luftwaffe's aircraft. Hence, in late October the Wehrmacht authorized the formation of the Condor Legion, originally comprising four twelve-plane squadrons of converted Junkers 52s, and a fighter group, made up of four nine-plane squadrons of Heinkel 51s. Early the following year, 1937, just as the cumbersome and poorly armed Junkers began to become an easy target for the Russian I-15 fighter – a powerful, snub-nosed biplane that could fly at 350 km/h (220 mph) before swooping down to attack (and which, coincidentally, had downed the 'Maxim Gorki' two years earlier) – the complement was strengthened by the welcome arrival of the newly developed bombers.

In the spring of 1935, and after years of denials, Hitler had publicly proclaimed the existence of the Luftwaffe. The top priority was the development of a medium bomber with a range of up to 1,500 km (1,000 miles), a payload of up to 2,200 pounds, and a speed of at least 320 km/h. Since no existing prototype satisfied all the criteria, the air force, or Luftwaffe, chose to develop three, all of which doubled as airliners. The first, the Junkers 86, was plagued by fundamental design problems and, although several hundred examples were built, it would never play an important part in the Luftwaffe's war plans. A second, more successful design was the Dornier 17, known popularly as the 'Flying Pencil' and an adaptation of a high-speed passenger plane commissioned for and then rejected by Lufthansa on the grounds of impracticality: to reach its predicted speed of more than 320 km/h, its designers had to make the cabin so narrow that it could carry only six passengers. Once cast away by the airline, Luftwaffe took it on; although it could carry only one 250 kg (550 lb) bomb, the plane could fly faster than any fighter currently in service. A third medium bomber, the Heinkel 111, was also tailored for a civilian role, but its designers at least bore in mind the possibility of future military applications. As flown

by Lufthansa, the Heinkel 111 carried ten passengers in two cabins, between which lay an unusually large space – the smoking compartment. Naturally, in the aircraft's military configuration, this area accommodated a payload of four 550 lb bombs.[26]

In the spring of 1937, excepting the railway station, a gun factory on the outskirts and a road bridge leading south-west toward Bilbao, the market town of Guernica in northern Spain contained few structures that could be regarded as of military significance. However, to the Basques (who know it as Gernika) it held much that was politically important, for here, under the huge oak tree whose dead and weathered trunk had become a virtual shrine to the cause of ethnic liberty, Spanish monarchs traditionally had come to pledge their respect for the local rights of the region's residents. And now, alarmingly, the northern theatre of the Spanish Civil War seemed about to converge on the sleepy town. Franco's

Prior to its service in Spain, the Heinkel 111 was also used by Lufthansa as a high-speed mail carrier.

Nationalist troops were approaching from the south while Republican troops were falling back toward Bilbao; many of them would need to cross the Oca river by way of Guernica's compact stone bridge.

At 4.30 pm on 26 April, as farmers and market-traders carried on business in the central square, the church bell rang to announce incoming planes. The inhabitants took cover in cellars, under bridges and in makeshift shelters. A few minutes later the lead aircraft, a brand new Heinkel 111, arrived fast and furious, dropping its load: over a ton of high explosive. For the next three hours the bombers following – more Heinkels and Junkers 52s, known to the Republicans as 'Trams' – released their destructive cargoes upon the cowering town. An early hit sheared away the front wall of the Julian Hotel, exposing four floors; soon afterwards a large section of the railway station was demolished; sporadic explosions levelled rows of wooden buildings, and, most grievously, the town's hospitals were hit: sick children, wounded soldiers and the medical staff who cared for them died together. In later sorties the warplanes began to drop incendiaries, an ordnance then largely untested. Silver tubes, the size of a forearm, but heavier, since they contained thermite and magnesium, glistened like tinsel in the early evening light, before crashing down through rooftops, fracturing on contact and disgorging a molten metal that ripped through wooden floor to wooden floor, igniting each timber it touched. Residents struggled out of their cellars as buildings burning above now began to collapse on top of them. Once on the streets they were targeted by the Heinkel 51 fighters that appeared suddenly out of the clouds of smoke billowing over the roofs. Ugly little biplanes, pin-nosed and split-wheeled, their pilots strapped low in open cockpits, they flew low, strafing the pavement with their front-mounted heavy machine-guns, cutting down men, women, children and animals as they ran for refuge. As the bombs continued to fall and the town burned on, the pall of smoke, ash and dust rose so thick that the later flights had to come in below 600 feet in order to distinguish the town from the countryside.[27]

At dusk, about 7.45 pm, when the last wave of bombers departed, much of Guernica had been razed, and its ruins were still smoking the following morning when foreign journalists arrived at the scene. George Steer, the *Times*'s famous reporter, claimed to hear 'the nervous crackle of arson' throughout the town, before the extent of the carnage became clear: 'the total furnace that was Guernica began to play tricks of crimson colour with the night clouds.'[28] The survivors gleaned in the rubble for remains of friends, relatives and belongings; it was thought that as many as 1,600 people had perished. Three-quarters of the town's dwellings were destroyed, the rest were seriously damaged. And yet despite the intensity of the bombardment, several obvious targets remained standing: the munitions factory was virtually untouched; the Basque oak still stood; and the little stone bridge was intact.

The Condor Legion's failure to destroy Guernica's military targets underlined a basic flaw in German weapons technology at the time. All the new heavy bombers in the Luftwaffe shared a complicated bomb-sight that needed extensive practice before it could be relied upon to deliver the payload accurately. Within a year or two, a simpler and more reliable device would be introduced, but in the interim, concern for precision led the Luftwaffe to accelerate the development of a *Sturzkampfflugzeug*, or 'diving attack plane', a term which, when applied to the Junkers 87, would be shortened to the evocative Stuka. This ungainly single-engined warplane, with limited range and load, and whose distinctively upward-slanted wings made it glacially slow in level flight, nevertheless

possessed phenomenal accuracy, which perfectly suited it for the destruction of vital tactical targets such as bridges, factories and gun emplacements that might be missed by heavier bombers flying at higher altitudes.

The theory of dive bombing was simple: since the First World War pilots had understood that, taking into account relative windspeed, any plane aimed vertically over the target prior to releasing its bombs should score a bull's-eye every time, the lateral speed of the plane being zero in relation to the target, and the force of gravity acting on the bomb being compounded by the airspeed of the plane. As it happened, Stuka pilots seldom achieved vertical dives, although they often plummeted at 80 degrees, which generally proved accurate enough. Certainly the crews required *Sturzmut* –'dive nerve' – to hurtle toward the ground in this fashion, watching the landscape below grow larger with dizzying speed, before the pilot levered down the drilled metal air brakes under the wings to slow the headlong dive, the

The gull-winged Junkers Ju-87 *Stuka* was dreaded by those troops and civilians subjected to its dive-bombing attacks.

whistle of the air passing through them compounding the terrible cacophony.[29] For, as his plane plunged earthward, the whine of its propeller was usually accompanied by a high-pitched scream as the sirens attached to the spatted landing gear began rotating; most Stukas were equipped with these sirens, known as Trumpets of Jericho, which the two-man crew felt added an extra *Freude* to the impetus of their attacks. At about 900 metres (3,000 ft) the pilot would release the 250 kg (550 lb) bomb harnessed to the plane's fuselage, the Stuka losing an additional 450 metres (1,500 ft) of altitude before levelling off and climbing back to return to base, mission over, joining the other 'Junker angels in the sky'.[30]

The plane, unperfected in Spain, would quickly prove itself when allied to the Blitzkrieg tactic deployed in Poland in September 1939, virtually obliterating an entire infantry division at Piotrków station, and destroying all but two of the Polish warships. Its accuracy was perfectly complemented by the more intense firepower offered by its strike partners, the Dornier and the Heinkel, which began the bombing of Warsaw with an attack on the PZL aircraft factory, the fires from which quickly engulfed neighbouring civilian properties. Yet despite its success, the Blitzkrieg proved costly to the Luftwaffe: four hundred aircraft had been lost or damaged by the Polish Air Force. Since the Stukas were heavy, slow to manoeuvre, poorly armed and vulnerable to frontal attack, losses, even to the lightly armed Polish biplanes, were substantial.

In 1941 a German feature film, directed by Karl Ritter, was made about the aircraft, and included a famous scene in which Bork, the squadron leader, addresses his pilots, lined up before their machines, and tells them of the dangers involved in the imminent Battle of Britain. As the camera zooms in to reveal the hard edges of their faces, and the image dissolves into the clouds, the pilots begin to sing:

Always prepared and ready to attack
[track-in to happy, smiling faces and a Stuka formation]
We the Stukas, Stukas, Stukas.
We dive from the sky
[more resolute, but happy faces]
We advance on – to defeat England.

Howard Smith, an American diplomat who happened to see *Stukas* in Berlin in 1941, described it as 'a monotonous film about a bunch of obstreperous adolescents who dive bombed things and people. They bombed everything and everybody. That was all the film was – one bombing after another'.[31] As it happened, *Stukas*

Alfred Hierl, *Stuka Pilots* (1942).

was a concerted piece of special pleading, given the aircraft's failure over southern England in 1940, where it was hopelessly inadequate against the swifter Spitfires and Hurricanes. Certainly, Stukas screamed from the sky, as before, but now most were unable to pull up before they smashed into the ground.

In fact, within three years of its introduction, not just the Stuka, but all the German bombing fleet would be found wanting; furthermore, there were no new designs in the offing. The reason perhaps stems from an apocryphal comment made by Goering: 'The Führer', he told an aide, 'does not ask me what kind of bombers I have. He wants to know only how many.'[32] Whatever the number of aircraft lost, the economies of scale at the heart of the Nazi war machine would ensure that replacements were always quickly in place. By 1943, however, the options were narrowing. Though Hitler was eager to develop the *Amerikabomber*, a long-range machine to strike at the Eastern seaboard of the United States, there was little opportunity for Messerschmitt to develop such a technologically advanced venture beyond a prototype. Instead, resources were re-directed from the company's other projects, such as its Me 262 fighter, the revolutionary jet-propelled machine that could touch 870 km/h (540 mph) when the fastest contemporary Allied fighter, the Rolls-Royce powered Mustang, could manage only 710 km/h (440 mph). In November 1943 an Me 262 was flown to Hitler's headquarters, the Wolf's Lair, then at Insterburg (now Chernyakhovsk) in East Prussia, for inspection. Impressed, the Führer demanded immediate mass production of the aircraft, but as a bomber, to be named *Sturmvogel* (Stormbird) and capable of carrying two 500 kg (1,100 lb) bombs or a single 1,000 kg (2,200 lb) projectile. However, as it would have to carry these weapons externally, its speed advantage over Allied piston-engined fighters would be lost immediately.

Willy Messerschmitt, the firm's founder, dumbfounded at the suggestion, nevertheless proposed schemes to enable the Me 262 to fulfil its bombing role without drastic alteration. One of the most ambitious proposals was to fly with a 900 kg (2,000 lb) bomb, fitted with wooden wings, in tow, attached to the jet with a rigid bar. The plan called for the *Sturmvogel*'s pilot to attack his target in a shallow dive and then release the bomb, explosive bolts shearing off the tow-bar and the bomb's wings. However, the flight trials proved difficult: the bomb's airfoils had been designed with too much lift, causing it to porpoise wildly and making the towing jet so uncontrollable that one test pilot had to bale out. In any event, in November 1944, faced with escalating USAF daylight bombing raids, Hitler rescinded his order and demanded the immediate construction of thousands of Me 262 fighters – although adding, to save face, that, like the Reich's beloved Stuka, this jet-powered machine must be capable of carrying at least one small 250 kg (550 lb) bomb.

The Messerschmitt Me 262, Germany's first operational jet fighter-bomber, was perhaps the finest airframe of the Second World War, but was hampered by its unreliable Jumo engines. This version has been fitted with an ungainly radar aerial array.

Castles in the Air

When Churchill met Roosevelt at a summit meeting at Quebec in August 1943, the British Prime Minister requested that a recently released Disney cartoon be laid on for the US President's entertainment. Neither *Dumbo* nor *Saludos Amigos* was projected through the leaders' Havana smoke that evening, but rather *Victory Through Air Power*, a feature-length film presenting the theories of Major Alexander de Seversky, whose best-selling book of the same title had appeared the previous year. A Russian émigré, amputee (he lost his leg when his Russian aircraft was shot down on his first combat flight) and onetime head of the Republic aircraft company, (makers of the P-47 Thunderbolt), de Seversky claimed to have written the book in an attempt to alert the American people to the immense opportunities air power offered, but also to the fact that the nation's leaders remained in ignorance of them. Later, explaining his adaptation of the book, Disney claimed to have been deeply interested in aviation for several years, sensing, like de Seversky, 'that air power held the key to the outcome of this war'. And even though he believed he would probably lose money on the film, he announced: 'I'm concerned that America should see it, and now is no time to think of personal profits.'[33]

As it happened, the film, which opened on 17 July 1943, cost US$788,000 to make and grossed US$799,000, turning a minor profit and also garnering an Academy Award. Its publicity materials announcing 'There's a Thrill in the Air', *Victory Through Air Power* opens with an engrossing cartoon version of the history of flight prior to the Second World War, and then, after 20 minutes, switches to live action in the form of de Seversky's talking head, shown in his office surrounded by world maps, aircraft models and blueprints. In his still thick White Russian accent, he sets out his message of air power and its importance to modern war, his presentation illustrated throughout by Disney's compelling and colourful graphics. In one sequence, Nazi Germany is presented as a huge iron wheel, at the hub of which great factories churn out arms and munitions, which are then distributed along the spokes to be used, eventually, around the thick circular rim. Allied armies tap away at the edge, the theatre of conflict, attacking tanks and planes, here and there, but the cunning Nazi axis reacts by simply rotating war material from one spoke to another, so countering the short-term threat. Hence, de Seversky suggests, the rim, the German machine, may too strong to be fractured by conventional armies or navies. However, fleets of allied aircraft then attack the factories of the hub directly, destroying them and causing the spokes to weaken and, as the wheel rolls on, the rim to collapse.

In another memorable sequence depicting the war in Asia, Disney figured Japan as an octopus whose tentacles are stretched across the Pacific, encircling dozens of helpless islands. Allied armies and navies attempt to chop through these sucking tentacles to liberate the islands, but it is futile. Only when the sharp claws of USAAF airpower, represented, naturally, by an American eagle, repeatedly strikes the bulbous head of the octopus, does the cephalopod release its hold on its outlying possessions and attempt to defend itself; but the effort is useless, and eventually it perishes under the attacks. As this is a cartoon, the violence is predictably, and grievously, sanitized. James Agee, reviewing the film, noted with unease that 'there are no suffering and dying enemy civilians under all those proud promised bombs; no civilians at all in fact'.[34]

At the time de Seversky began his book, the American Air Force was poorly equipped with bombers.[35] The Boeing B-17 'Flying Fortress', developed sporadically throughout the 1930s, became the mainstay of the Eighth Air Force in Europe, performing

high-altitude daylight bombing over Germany between 1942 and 1945, and suffering crippling losses to flak and fighters. The machine was solid enough, and popular with flight crews, but was hampered throughout its career by a small payload and, more seriously, a poor range. It was clear that, if the US was to defeat the tentacles of Japan, it needed a bomber with greater range. Boeing responded with the B-29 'Superfortress', the largest and most complex aircraft built in quantity during the Second World War, employing the biggest engines, the most sophisticated radar and bomb-sighting, and the most advanced fire-control system to deliver the greatest range and the heaviest bomb load. To create this, 12 tonnes (27,000 lb) of sheet aluminium, more than 450 kg (1,000 lb) of copper, 600,000 rivets, about 14 km (9 miles) of wiring and 3 km (2 miles) of tubing were required. It was appropriate that a machine of such complexity should drop the

The complex Boeing B-29 Superfortress was designed to perform precision bombing at high altitudes in daylight. Its fortunes were mixed in this role, and it was only when it was tasked to fly sorties at low altitude and at night that its devastating possibilities emerged.

bombs that, it seemed, would end war in Japan and, perhaps, begin a colder one.

Early on the morning of 6 August 1945, a series of six B-29s took off from Tinian Air Force Base. The first three were unarmed observation aircraft, but the fourth out, at 02.45, was the *Enola Gay*, commanded by Paul Tibbets and named after his mother. It carried in its aluminium belly the 'Little Boy', a uranium-fuelled atomic bomb, which was armed a quarter of an hour after take-off. Weather over the target, the industrial city of Hiroshima, was clear with unlimited visibility, just as had been predicted. At 08.15 Japanese time the bomb was delivered on Hiroshima from 9,600 metres (31,600 ft), exactly according to plan: the device detonated 43 seconds after release, when 500 metres (1,900 ft) above the ground, 210 metres (700 ft) from the aiming point, and with a force of 12.5 kilotons.

Thrilled by the accuracy of the raid, the planners looked for another window of opportunity in the changeable weather system then sitting over Japan. Three days later, on 9 August, a second B-29 named *Bockscar*, piloted by Major Charles Sweeney, the 393rd squadron commander, was chosen to carry the 'Fat Man', a plutonium device. Its crew had flown the observation aircraft, the *Great Artiste*, on 6 August and would now see a second explosion. However, unlike the Hiroshima mission, this one was plagued with problems and its unexpected outcome showed the random nature even of strategic bombing. First an inoperative pump trapped several hundred gallons of fuel in one of the wings, then a rendezvous between the bombing aircraft and two observation aircraft off Kyushu was mistimed, leaving *Bockscar* circling in a holding pattern for 45 minutes. And then the weather closed in on the entire operation: haze and smoke protected the primary target, Kokura, so, as ten Japanese fighters climbed toward the B-29,

Sweeney flew to the target next down the list, Nagasaki. Again dogged by heavily clouded weather conditions, but now with some assistance from the radar operator, the aircraft began its run until, at last, the aimer sighted the city through a small break in the clouds and released the bomb. 'Fat Man' exploded with double the force of the Hiroshima bomb, some distance from the intended aiming point. The mushroom cloud grew, After one quick circuit of the stricken city, *Bockscar* flew directly to Okinawa to make an emergency landing, its engine starved of fuel. Shortly after the event, one of Sweeney's crew compared the two blasts:

> There I was . . . looking out at a technicolor world and technicolor sky. The ball of fire was greater this time, wider and reaching higher into the sky, and the smoke was thicker and blacker and seemed to rise even more rapidly than it had at Hiroshima, and the colors, the browns, the purples, the greens, the yellows, the reds, were brighter. Huge rings of smoke, the circumference of which reached around most of the city, reached hungrily upward.[36]

Since the bombing is rendered in such vividly colourful cinematic terms, it's possible that the writer had seen the similarly garish representations of bomb explosions in Disney's film.

Despite such achievements, even the Superfortress was not the machine de Seversky had in mind for the Air Force when he wrote his book in 1942. He argued that since the USAF lacked an ultra long-range bomber it had become too reliant on overseas airbases. Consequently, as a means of reducing the nation's dependency on such vulnerable facilities, de Seversky pushed for the development of 'inter-hemispheric' bombers that could strike the enemy from the mainland of the United States. The machines visualized by Disney are not dissimilar to the Avro Lancaster in form – four-engined

and twin-tailed – but are considerably larger and, based in Alaska, they fly across the ice cap to pummel Japan relentlessly. The bombers do not require the usual fighter escort, but instead bristle with radar-controlled machine-guns, which down countless enemy interceptors.

Such a machine would only come into being once the war was over in the form of the Convair B-36 'Peacemaker', perhaps the world's first 'inter-hemispheric' bomber. When first envisaged in early 1941, before the US joined the war, this massive machine was intended to fly across the Atlantic, enter German airspace at 450 km/h (300 mph), and drop 4.5 tonnes (10,000 lb) of bombs from 40,000 feet, too high for flak or fighters to trouble it, before returning to the US. However, owing to design problems and also the demands of war production, it was only in June 1948 that Convair was able to deliver the first operational model; as well as the speed and range originally planned, it could haul a bomb load of 32 tonnes (72,000 lb) into the clouds.

Large as the B-29 was, a 'Superfortress' could almost nestle beneath one wing of a B-36. There were similarities: despite the

The Convair B-36 'Peacemaker', still the largest combat aircraft to have served with any air force, needed a crew of fifteen, including four reliefs, to fly it.

size difference, the two aircraft had similarly shaped vertical tails, slim fuselages, round in cross-section, with two pressurized crew cabins separated by two bomb bays and connected by a tunnel. But the wings were different, the Superfortress's thin, sharp and glider-like, while those of the B-36, 70 m (230 ft) in span, were more than seven feet thick at the root, large enough for a crewman to crawl in and reach the engines or the landing-gear in flight. The B-36 looked intimidatingly odd: its wings tapered sharply, and its leading edges were swept back, aerodynamic features that, combined with the wings' positioning far down the fuselage, made the aircraft appear ill-proportioned. Most bizarre of all, its six propeller engines were buried into the rear of the wing, the spinners facing backwards to push, rather than draw, the aircraft through the air. Such a configuration was rarely used by this time, but it worked here to ensure that the B-36 would have minimal drag in the thinner air of high altitudes. Later jet engines would be added to the outside edges, to increase still further speed and ceiling. However, the most striking feature was the ornate plexiglas canopy enclosing the flight deck, which, while ample for the four pilots and engineers needed to control the plane in flight, was tiny for such a massive plane that also carried another 11 airmen in its long fuselage. A bulge below the nose housed a radar antenna, and two transparent blisters allowed the crew to aim the guns and observe any mechanical problems in the wings or under-side. The aesthetic effect of the B-36, head-on, has been described as resembling 'a face like a prairie dog's peering from a burrow, with the flight deck for eyes, the scanning blisters for ears, and the radome for tucked-up paws'.[37]

The B-36 'Peacemaker' quickly became the mainstay of Strategic Air Command (SAC), a massive force of bombers and ballistic missiles under the leadership of General Curtis Le May,

ready at a moment's notice to unleash atomic weapons on the enemies of the US, or NATO, under the motto 'Peace is Our Profession'. On the Peacemaker's retirement from front-line duty in 1958, it would be noted that its name had encapsulated its achievements in the decade since its introduction. For despite the increasing chill of the Cold War and Europe and Korea at this time, this aircraft never went to war, never dropped a bomb in anger, nor even discharged its 16 remotely controlled 20 mm cannons at aircraft approaching too closely. This cannot be said of its successor, the B-52 'Stratofortress', first flown in April 1952 and, with some modifications and refitting, still in service fifty years later.

The B-52's advantage over the Peacemaker was, quite simply, speed. In late 1948 Boeing, flushed by the success of the B-47 jet, quietly dropped plans for a large but sluggish turboprop bomber and proposed instead a massive swept-wing aircraft, powered by

The eight-engine Boeing B-52 Stratofortress was first flown in 1952, and remains in the service of the USAF to this day.

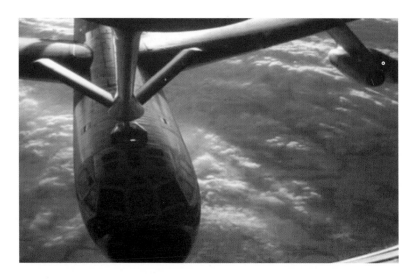

eight turbojet engines slung in four pods beneath the wings. Such a configuration would give the aircraft a cruising speed of more than 965 km/h (600 mph) and a range of 10,000 km (6,000 miles), which could easily be doubled with new air-to-air refuelling procedures. Once the B-52 came into service, SAC crews nicknamed it BUFF (the acronym allegedly spelling out 'Big Ugly Fat Fuck'). Though certainly big, and fat – the plane's enormous bomb bays could carry over 9 tonnes (20,000 lb), twice the capacity of its smaller sibling, the B-47 – the charge of ugliness was arguable. Despite the fact that the SAC B-52 he described was named 'Leper Colony', and armed with two thermonuclear weapons, the novelist Peter George nevertheless felt that, 'aesthetically the exterior shape of the aeroplane was pleasing. The swept wings gave an impression of arrow swiftness; the shining body, of brightness and cleanness; the eight great engines, of power and pure functional efficiency'.[38] However, as Kubrick's adaptation of George's novel *Dr Strangelove, or How I Learned to Stop Worrying and Love the Bomb* makes clear, these

The B-52 was fundamental to Strategic Air Command. In-flight refuelling allowed the bomber to remain on patrol for many hours, hugging the nap of the earth.

sophisticated and terrible aircraft are nothing other than 'fucks'; or, at the very least, sexual objects. The opening sequence shows 'fornicating flying machines', a B-52 being refuelled by a KC-135 tanker, the great boom ready to pump kerosene nuzzling and then penetrating the smooth surface of the Stratofortress. Inside, the crew fiddle with the contents of the emergency ration packs – gum, condoms, lipsticks, nylons – or look at *Playboy*; even the inside of the door of the safe, in which the SAC attack codes are secured, is decorated with images of Hefner's bunnies. And in the aircraft's belly, safe and insulated, sit the two bombs, ready to be delivered to mother Russia; one is labelled 'Hi There', the other, more apologetically for the end of someone's world, 'Dear John'. For many of the film's flying sequences, Kubrick and the film's designer, Ken Adam, had to rely on scale models, painstakingly created on the basis of the limited information on the aircraft then available in the public domain. Perhaps because of this, this famous satire of dehumanization succeeds in making the aircraft appear almost human; certainly more so that the film's protagonists.[39]

In the cockpit: a still from Stanley Kubrick's *Dr Strangelove* (1963).

Despite its continued success in SAC, the B-52 achieved greater notoriety for a combat role for which it was never intended: the high-altitude carpet bombing of guerrilla positions in several south-east Asian countries, commanded first by Johnson and then stepped up by Nixon on his assumption of the Presidency in 1968. Over 6.3 million tons of bombs fell on Vietnam, Laos and Cambodia during the war years; just over a third of that amount defeated the Third Reich and the Japanese Empire thirty years earlier. However, the apotheosis of the B-52 came in Operation Linebacker, authorized by Nixon in May 1972 in the context of a major North Vietnamese Army offensive against the South and a stalemate at the Paris peace talks. The first stage of the operation, through the summer, demanded that B-52s venture into heavily defended North Vietnamese airspace to stage night attacks on air-fields and oil-storage facilities, and also to lay mines in the waters of Haiphong and other strategic ports. By October 1972, when it seemed that the Paris talks were at last leading to an agreement that would end the war, air operations over North Vietnam were once more halted. However, when the peace talks again broke down amid indications that the North Vietnamese were preparing to renew their offensive in the South, 'Linebacker' resumed on 19 December with an eleven-day bombing campaign against the North that developed into the heaviest air offensive seen since the war in Japan. In addition to the principal North Vietnamese Air Force fighter bases and missile sites, the attacks by day and night were also directed at civilian targets that until then had been officially off limits to the USAF: railway yards, power stations, telecommunications facilities. The target list numbered over thirty strategic objectives, over 60 per cent of which were situated within a 25-mile radius of Hanoi, with the consequences imagined by June Jordan: 'shit tore forth / pouring from the b-52 bowels loose over Hanoi and the skin /and the agonized the blown limbs the blinded eyes the / silence of the children dead on the street'.[40] In the eleven days of the campaign, 729 B-52 sorties were flown and more than 15,000 tons of bombs were dropped on 34 targets, with the loss of some 1,500 civilians. Nevertheless, the cost to the US was substantial too, as fifteen B-52s, costing $40 million each, were lost to missiles, and nine damaged, before North Vietnam announced that it was ready to resume peace negotiations.

The B-52s then flew away from Vietnam, never to return, and many military analysts believed that, given the gradual shift to cruise missiles, 'Linebacker' had signalled the twilight of the career of this behemoth.[41] The aircraft, however, returned to action once more in 1991, cheaply crushing Iraq's Republican Guard. And then, ten years later, when surgical strikes and 'smart bombs' had failed to dislodge Osama bin Laden from the Tora Bora cave complex, they were called in to pulverize the mountains with heavy metal and napalm, dropped from castles in the air.

Stealth Tactics

Through sparkling visibility the bombers came to the city, outspread, unsleeping, on the bright Tuesday in early September. Twin-aisled, wide-bodied Boeings both, American and United, silver and dark blue, they delivered their cargo at intervals into the heart of the world. Twenty minutes earlier, America, in its Pacific, Mountain, Central and Eastern time zones, tuned in as ever to the breakfast show, at first thought the breaking news was nothing more serious than the most bizarre air crash in the nation's history: an American Airlines 767, *en route* to LA had by some means succeeded in burying itself in the north tower of the World Trade Center, between the 94th and the 99th floors. Aircraft had struck New York's skyscrapers before: in 1945, lost in the fog covering Manhattan island, a Boeing B-25 bomber had pierced the Empire State Building at the 78th floor, killing fourteen people; the iron-framed tower had barely trembled. But this time, the technology of the accident was more advanced. The Trade Center towers had been engineered only to withstand the impact of a 707, the largest plane at the time of the building's conception in the late 1960s; but the 767 was a bigger aircraft with a longer range, spun out of the research Boeing had carried out for its Jumbo programme. It carried more fuel and had now, in addition to its kinetic energy, deposited 31,000 litres of kerosene into the heart of the north tower of the complex.

Twenty minutes later, as a second, darker 767 approached the south tower, the world now watching on television suddenly saw the potential terrors that air transport contained; a two-engined, wide-bodied airliner – an object familiar from business meetings and Thanksgiving travels, and made by a trusted firm whose corporate slogan at the time was 'Bringing People Together' – transformed into a bomber. That second plane, tanked up for a long flight from Boston to Los Angeles, spooled up its turbofans as it passed the Statue of Liberty and at full thrust, a couple of hundred metres above Battery Park at the southern tip of Manhattan, banked left as it lined up with the unscathed tower. The Boeing now seemed less an example of America's industrial expertise than an object wholly military, which was striking the south tower of the WTC with the force of a tactical nuclear device. The edifice of glass and steel was 50 metres (160 ft) deep. It took roughly six-tenths of a second for the jet, travelling at more than 600 km/h (400 mph), to come to rest inside, for the inferno to fall out of the other side of the building, into the blue; and for America to have a sense of the firepower visiting her from seemingly innocent civilian technology.

Yet the 767s here in New York, along with the other two Boeing jets that gunned into the Pentagon or dropped on Pennsylvanian farmland, were being aimed at the nation's vision of itself, and of its war machine. Once on board the wide-bodied Boeings, the terrorists would have been comfortable in the knowledge that they had been built by the nation's largest defence contractor; as several of them had trained as pilots they might even have been aware that 767 airframes would soon form the backbone of the USAF's new tanker fleet. Hence the curious serendipity of the attack, which proved, as nothing else, that the nation's mastery of the air achieved over the previous half century was, on 11 September 2001 at least, illusory. For the previous half century, the nation's aerial power, as vested in the relentless potency of the B-52, or its air defence, symbolized by the lethality of its missile systems, seemed to guarantee the possibility of 'limited war', a conflict only ever fought on the United States' terms: at the President's behest, under his control. Moreover, imagery of the instant hit of an air strike was visually appealing; for if statistics are unconfirmed, or hard facts unappetizing, grainy sequences of 'smart bombs' disappearing into air-conditioning ducts with the minimum of 'collateral damage' were compensation enough for analysis, and could be replayed on the networks *ad nauseam*. But as Clausewitz noted in *On War*, 'War is an act of force – which can theoretically have no limits'; trying to confine conflict to a given geographical area in an era of global communication is to risk both defeat and a misunderstanding of the nature of the enemy. And that morning, Mohammed Atta and his fellow terrorists showed not simply that the theatre of war could not be confined, but that it could go undetected until the point of detonation.

Ironically, it was not so much bombers but surveillance aircraft that had allowed the emergence of a sense that, if an enemy cannot

be seen, it cannot threaten. In the years after the Second World War, the US had gathered aerial intelligence by removing the weapons from a fighter or bomber, stuffing it full of cameras and assigning it the prefix 'R' for 'reconnaissance'. But in late 1953, with Soviet nuclear weapons, ballistic missiles, and attendant economic and military structures hidden behind a heavily defended curtain, a need for aircraft designed specifically to perform long-range aerial surveillance was recognized, and so 'spy planes' such as the U-2 were developed to bombard the enemy, not with ordnance but with scrutiny. Optimized for very high flight, the Utility Plane 2 was essentially a high-powered glider, able to soar at altitudes of 23,000 m (75,000 ft), with a range exceeding 7,400 km (4,600 miles). In its nose it carried a sophisticated camera, known as the Type B, which carried over a mile of custom made, ultra-thin Eastman Kodak film, which, even so, weighed around 136 kg (300 lb) and which, to maintain the airplane's centre of gravity, needed to be spooled on a pair of nine-inch-wide rolls feeding in opposite directions on parallel tracks. The aircraft was quite literally a winged lens; it was also unpredictable in its handling characteristics and prone to stalling in thin air. Furthermore, its long wings made it difficult to land in one piece; hence, Don De Lillo memorably describes the 'black-bandit jet' in *Libra*, and its distinctive final approaches: 'It had a balsa-wood lightness, a wobbliness, uncommonly long-winged', and it came

Originally a spy plane operated by the CIA with cover provided by the civilian NACA, the Lockheed U-2 became the most controversial aircraft of its time.

to earth 'sweet-falling, almost feathery, dependent on winds, sailing on winds'.[42]

For nearly four years after its introduction in 1956, the Russian Air Defences could detect, but were impotent against, the regular intrusions of this 'utility plane' into the nation's vast airspace, until on the morning of 1 May 1960, a fortnight before a superpower summit conference in Paris, there appeared over Sverdlovsk, a large industrial area in the Urals, a black aircraft with enormous drooping wings and a peculiarly large tail, on which was painted in large white letters 'U-2'. After crash landing, Francis Gary Powers, the pilot, presented his credentials to the authorities: two military identification cards, US and International driver's licences, a Social Security card, a medical certificate, two flying licences, currency in American dollars and five other denominations, two Rolex watches, gold coins and seven gold rings, which, as Khrushchev later suggested, must have been 'for the ladies'. Along with his pistol with a silencer, morphine and flares, he also carried a 'large silk American flag poster' in fourteen languages reading: 'I am an American and do not speak your language. I need food, shelter and assistance. I will not harm you. I bear no malice toward your people. If you help me, you will be rewarded.' Eisenhower promised to abandon further flights across the USSR; a recent, plausible suggestion, however, is that the pilot, or the aircraft, was expected to be identified, brought down and displayed so that a conference considered undesirable by the US might more easily be cancelled.[43]

In any event, two years later another U-2 mission created a diplomatic incident. A U-2 overflying Cuba in October 1962 had returned with photos showing compelling evidence of Soviet surface-to-surface missiles capable of reaching many strategic and industrial targets in the United States. The images were stark and unambiguous: nine emplacements were visible in four separate locations, intelligence specialists concluding that the weapons were fitted with nuclear warheads and could reach as far west as Wyoming and Montana. Their presence, and that of a force of Ilyushin IL-28 light bombers, represented a major increase of Soviet firepower in the Caribbean and broke promises that President Kennedy assumed the Russians had made to him earlier. A few days later, a U-2 on another intelligence-gathering flight over the island was downed by a surface-to-air missile, killing the pilot, Rudolf Anderson. Meanwhile yet another U-2, engaged on what was described as a high-altitude sampling flight over the Arctic, became lost and entered Russian airspace. MiGs were scrambled to intercept, as the USAF managed to escort the errant spy plane back to Alaska. Twice in a single day, this singular aircraft had brought America and the Soviet Union to the brink of war; and over the next few weeks Kennedy placed his nation's military forces on alert, as SAC Stratofortresses maintained a continuously airborne status. A naval blockade of Cuba stopped further missile deliveries, Russia agreed to withdraw other missiles from the island, and the crisis subsided. The incident, however, dramatized the key role of surveillance aircraft in a world threatened with destruction by intercontinental jet bombers.

In the late 1960s there emerged a new version, the U-2R, a larger and slightly heavier machine whose performance at altitude was transformed by the development of a wing of greater span and area. First flown on 28 August 1967, this model remains in service more than thirty years later; clearly, the imagery of the former Soviet Union in the late 1980s must have suggested that the US might soon be omnipotent, as well as omniscient. Yet since the fading of the Communist bloc the imagery has, perhaps, been less clear cut. Indeed, Nicholson Baker's flippant suggestion that 'the Cold

War has moved from the upper atmosphere of spy photography to the wind tunnel, and aerodynamic drag has effectively replaced the Soviet Union as the infinitely resourceful enemy' may pass close to the truth.[44] Certainly, it would explain the US's obsession over the last fifteen years or so with bringing into service the Advanced Technology Bomber, a machine whose extraordinary design features render it invisible, at least to electronic detection if not to prying cameras, and account for its cost of $1.3 billion per plane.

When they began work on the bomber that would eventually become known as the B-2 'Spirit', Northrop's engineers proposed a form that, although radically different from those of comparable modern bombers, clearly echoed the spirit, if not the substance, of

The Northrop XB-35, a massive all-wing bomber, made its first flight in 1946, but suffered from stability problems. Later, it would provide the template for the B-2 Spirit.

the 'Flying Wing' designs for which the company had become famous just after the Second World War. Aerodynamically, such a form behaves very differently to aircraft with a slender fuselage and a tail unit, and theoretically should have a payload and range 25 per cent greater. Such shapes, though, are inherently unstable at lower speeds and, after several accidents in 1948, Northrop dropped researches in the later 1940s. Once the vogue for 'low observability', or 'stealth', surfaced in the early 1970s, however, it seemed that the wing might yet fly again.

Stealth technology emerged at that time when engineers at Lockheed started work on a fighter-bomber, eventually developed into the SR-71 Blackbird, with faceted surfaces to reflect and

The cockpit of a Lockheed SR-71 Blackbird, whose advanced aerodynamic design and structural features influenced later 'stealth' designs.

disperse radio waves, so making its radar signal vague. For once, aerodynamic considerations did not set the agenda that shaped the aircraft; instead, electronics held the key.[45] Since its wings are entirely moulded into the fuselage, such as it exists, and a tailplane has been eliminated altogether, the B-2 lacks those points of inter-section between planes that show up so starkly in radar signals. Its wing surfaces have been rounded off, and the cockpit, like a skate's head, has been carefully flattened into the wing, entirely made of the graphite-based, composite materials that make up half of the B-2's structure. The engines are drilled deeply into the body of the aircraft, and their inlets have been carefully concealed. The leading edge of the wing is designed to channel air into these shady inlets from all directions, and still secret 'radar-absorbent' materials are

A head-on view of the Northrop B-2 Spirit stealth bomber, brought into service in the late 1980s.

employed here to reduce even further radar reflectivity. The saw-tooth shape of the trailing edge helps screen engine exhaust gases, which already have been mixed into and cooled by ambient air.

Originally the USAF wanted 133 of these exotic machines, without question the most advanced aircraft ever built, but by 1991 successive budget cuts had reduced the order to just 21 aircraft. The first B-2 was delivered to the 393rd Bomb Squadron at Whiteman Air Force Base, Missouri, on 17 December 1993, and the type saw combat six years later in Kosovo, flying long transatlantic missions to deliver 'smart bombs' on high-priority objectives. The record, such as it exists, is impressive; the B-2s flew one per cent of the missions, but accounted for eleven per cent of all targets destroyed. Certainly, through such deployments as these, the ideology of bombing has moved away from deterrence towards pre-emptive 'surgical strikes' on targets such as installations housing (to stretch the jargon still further) 'weapons of mass destruction'. The air forces of the Cold War – the orbiting American Peacemakers and Stratofortresses, Russian Bears and Bisons, constant reminders of the relative security of Mutually Assured Destruction – were a guarantee that the world would not be turned into a radioactive desert; but now the airbrakes have broken away, and the world is diving towards unprecedented civilian terrors. And despite the fact that so much of the USAF budget was spent on such arcane and exotic designs as the Stealth Bomber, it seems that until the attacks of 11 September the Pentagon planners had not before realized that the skies of America were already full of potential stealth bombers, aircraft primed and ready to wreak mass destruction at the heart of the metropolis.

3 Silver Bullets

Plastic Visions

Things to Come begins in 1940 in Everytown, a barely disguised London, whose citizens are preparing for Christmas despite a threat of War suggested by the ubiquitous headlines: 'Alarming Speech by Air Minister'. In his gloomy study, Dr John Cabal, an eminent scientist, has discarded his newspaper and walks over to the hearth, in which the logs are blazing brightly; within days, bombs will be falling, filled with gas and high explosive, and the city will burn as brightly. Wells's highly prescriptive treatment of his novel had called for 'diagrams and models' to indicate Cabal's status as an engineer, suggesting that 'the blade of a propeller over the mantel and other objects [would] emphasize his association with the air force'.[1] In the event, the film's designer, the painter Vincent Korda, placed over the fireplace a much more distinctive icon: a painting of a Douglas DC-3, the Dakota, the most famous airliner aircraft in history, which had flown for the first time in late 1935, only a few months before the film was released. (*Flight Magazine* was impressed by such detailing: 'from the aeronautical point of view, apart from any other, congratulations are due to those responsible'.)[2]

Ironically, this epoch-making aircraft was not in itself a revolutionary design, but merely a careful evolution of recent aeronautical

A painting of a Douglas DC-3 takes pride of place over the fireplace in John Cabal's study. A still from *Things to Come* (1936).

innovations. The development of more powerful liquid-cooled engines at the end of the 1920s had led, naturally, to an intensification of cruising speeds, which in turn demanded a complementary shift in aircraft form. The old style of angular, skeletal airframe disappeared, to be replaced by softer and smoother organic forms, the ideal solution to the problem of wind resistance. Cockpits were now being enclosed by perspex blisters, stalky under-carriages were disappearing into underwing bays and, most importantly, bulky engines were being wrapped in smooth-edged fairings. Since the beginning of flight, aircraft motors had been left largely exposed to the elements in order to facilitate cooling. In 1928, however, Fred E. Weick, an engineer working for the US government's National Advisory Committee for Aeronautics (NACA), found that wrapping the engine in a cowl, open at the front and rear, would eliminate much of the drag and, more importantly, accelerate the cooling effect of air on the engine. While this new fairing was of little value on engines suspended below the wings – even the most streamlined cowling would not overcome the turbulence generated by such an arrangement – Weick proved, however, that if engines were sunk into the wing itself, into pods he termed 'nacelles', the performance gain was as tremendous as the advance in aesthetics.[3]

'They'll never build them any bigger', announced a Boeing engineer as the company's latest passenger transport, the 247, took to the sky over Seattle in February 1933, its stressed metal fuselage glistening in the sun and exhibiting the ultimate in streamlining techniques: the shape of things to come. The engines were mounted on the forward edge of the low-slung wing, enclosed in the nacelles, the two features combining to give the 247 a cruising speed 80–112 km/h (50–70 mph) faster than any other airliner of the time. In addition, it was the first airliner to be fitted with retractable landing-gear and a controllable pitch propeller. She had de-icing devices on the wings and tailplane to allow high-altitude cruising, was soundproofed, and was the first passenger aircraft to have an 'automatic pilot' installed – a third crew member to prevent pilot fatigue on longer stretches. The effect of these innovations was immediate and startling: even with seven stops across the continent, the 247 cut the coast-to-coast travel time from 27 hours to 19 hours.

It was this machine, then, that gave rise to the Douglas DC-3. Trans World Airlines (TWA), desperate to compete with United Airlines, whose exclusive order for 247s had tied up the Boeing production lines for several years, approached the Douglas Company, a flamboyant firm based in Santa Monica, California. Donald Douglas, the founder of the company, was given a brief by the chairman of TWA: the airline wanted a plane constructed

Boeing 247s on the production line, Seattle, 1932.

mainly of metal, though other materials could be used for certain components; to weigh no more than 6,450 kg (14,200 lb), and carry at least 12 passengers over a range of 1,750 km (1,080 miles), at a speed of at least 240 km/h (150 mph). Effectively, TWA was commissioning an alternative version of the 247, and legend has it that Douglas placed a large photograph of that machine in the office of the design team, bearing the caption: 'Like this. Only better'. They began with the DC-1, a single prototype, about 20 per cent bigger and 30 per cent heavier than the Boeing 247; crucially, its wing spars were placed beneath the floor-line, to leave an entirely unobstructed passenger cabin. Flight tests proved it to be immensely durable, if slightly underpowered, so the Douglas engineers lengthened it, fitted it with larger engines, and called it the DC-2; this machine would cruise at 275 km/h (170 mph), but was unwieldy in handling, 'a stiff legged brute'. The breakthrough came in late 1934, when the Douglas engineers widened and lengthened the fuselage, increased the size of the wing and tail section, and installed Wright Cyclone engines capable of propelling the machine to a cruising speed of 300 km/h (185 mph). They presented to its first customer a machine capable of carrying 21 passengers, and 50 per cent extra payload, for only 10 per cent extra cost.

To achieve this astonishing performance, the aircraft would make use of the most advanced streamlining technologies: the new wing's leading edge was swept back sharply, while the rear trailing edge was kept straight, to create a silhouette shaped like a coat hanger – aerodynamic perfection, nevertheless. Walter Dorwin Teague would later describe this distinctive aspect of the DC-3: 'This line, composed of a short parabolic curve and a long sweep, straight, or almost straight, expresses force and grace . . . There is surely no more exciting form in modern design.'[4] But at least part

of the success of the design was the obsessive attention to detail. Douglas, his fellow engineers claimed, had the ability to see the spray – that is, he could detect airflow without needing to gather evidence from a wind tunnel. He pored over the plans and rubbed out anything that would create drag. In previous versions, the door handles were already a streamlined if protuberant bullet-shape, and the rivets were rounded; in the DC-3, Douglas ordered that the handles be completely recessed, and the rivets flush with the surface. In this way, in the space of five years, the speed of air transport increased by about 80 per cent.

Speed, of course, was not everything. A remarkable demonstration of the aesthetic qualities of streamlined aircraft emerges from Le Corbusier's *Aircraft*, the fourth section of which bears the bold heading, 'A new state of modern conscience. A new plastic vision. A new aesthetic', after which the architect announces that the 'plasticians of the world are everywhere full of activity, energetic, innumerable, unlimited'.[5] Underneath these stark statements are two equally austere images, stills from the documentaries *Aero Engine* and *Contact*, made in 1932 by Paul Rotha for the GPO Film Unit – the first photograph depicting the cross-section of an airfoil, and the

The Douglas DC-3, which first entered service in 1935.

second the propeller assembly of an Armstrong-Siddeley Tiger engine under repair. Overleaf, four more film stills are neatly arranged, each taken from a low angle and with a restricted field of vision. Two depict the Fairey long-range Monoplane, a beautifully streamlined machine commissioned in 1933 by the Air Ministry for long-distance research work, and two the Armstrong-Whitworth Atalanta, a transport plane flown by Imperial Airways on freight and passenger services to colonies in Africa and the Far East. The effect is to refamiliarize rather than to defamiliarize, to make us aware of the 'harmonizing influence' between technology and nature. A series of whiskery slashes in the smooth muzzle of the Fairey Monoplane makes it look animalistic, canine, even; the single air inlet set into the great bulbous visage of the Atalanta threatens the observer, as any Cyclops might when bearing a spear in the form of a propeller blade. Another Atalanta is pictured head on, squatting perfectly symmetrical about the axis, ready to launch itself towards the camera. There are several other such abstracted images of aircraft in this section, and in each case the parts stand for the whole, a mechanical synecdoche that leads to an overpowering aggregate; a carefully calculated image of functional technology and aesthetic statement. For these aero-dynamic forms are by no means neutral at this point in Le Corbusier's career, since these aircraft, although covered by stressed skin, seem to herald another order of architectonic design, that of poured concrete, which he would use to great effect in many of his greatest post-war commissions, most notably the chapel at Ronchamp.[6]

The link between technological and the organic is made even clearer in the next chapter, in which Le Corbusier finally approaches the principles that much of *Aircraft* has so far circled around; the strategies of human organization that aerodynamic technology might imply. Hence, five images of aero and fluid

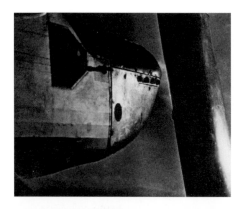

dynamics – the movement of viscous fluid behind a stationary cylinder, behind an obstacle, and round wing and spherical forms – face a page that carries the capitalized pronouncement: 'ALL THINGS IN LIFE ARE ORGANISMS.'[7] This sequence is later complemented by an image of a lake in the French Pyrenees – an aerial shot, taken from high altitude – which shows the path of the water across the terrain, a working together of current and course, to create a larger structure. Taken together, the implication might be that the least resistance in the component parts contributes to the smooth working of the whole. It is a suggestion

The nose of the Fairey long-range Monoplane and the Armstrong-Whitworth Atalanta, both excerpted from the film *Aero Engine* (1932) and subsequently featured in Le Corbusier's *Aircraft* (1935).

A head-on view of an Atalanta and another shot of the Fairey, the former from the film *Contact* (1933) and the latter from *Aero Engine*, both subsequently featuring in *Aircraft* (1935).

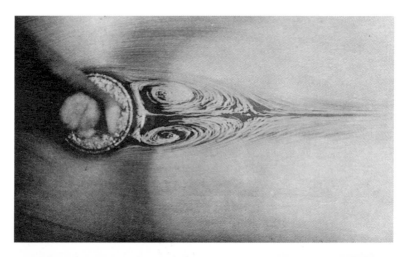

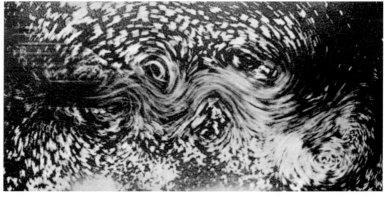

Aero- and hydrodynamics: a collage of photographs in *Aircraft* (1935).

that, given the epoch out of which the book emerged, raises the question of subordination and integration; of the relation between individual will and collective power. Inevitably the aircraft had become a model of such a new orderliness, a prototype of spatial organization, derived from its cognate, the organic. Some years later, Le Corbusier would claim that the Lockheed Constellation, the aircraft which he so admired, was beautiful because 'it is like a fish, it might have been like a bird'; in any case, it contained a new harmony of the technological with the natural.[8] The fact that machine civilization had developed alternative orders – most notably Fordism – is left unaddressed by *Aircraft*; instead Le Corbusier pushes through a concept of streamlining that channels the dynamic flow of natural elements into the smooth unfettered progress of modernity.

'Let's streamline men and women', proclaimed the designer Alexis de Sakhnoffsky in 1937; necessarily, this process would have affected the very form of the body.[9] J. G. Ballard has recently suggested, rather caustically, that 'streamlining satisfies the dream of flight without the effort of growing wings. Aerodynamics is the modern sculpture of non-Euclidean space–time'.[10] Hence, with the appearance of this new race, the difference between humans and machines would narrow; the Fourth Dimension could be attained, but only via the short cut of amputation. Toes were rejected as an artistic remnant of Neanderthal times, when men clambered in branches; ears were pinned back; the nose was flattened: aerodynamic efficiency became the key. After the cult of *Neue Sachlichkeit* and skeletal constructivism in the late 1920s, there was now an obsession with a body shaped and honed, strengthened and enjoyed, through activity; a body at one with a machine, swift and efficient.

In *Things to Come*, war is declared, and John Cabal joins the Air

Force to defend Everytown against the ranks of gas bombers massing over the White Cliffs of Dover. At the controls of a Hawker Fury biplane, one of the fastest British interceptors of the day, he downs an enemy fighter. Gallantly, he lands by the wreckage and pulls the pilot free, before disappearing into the skies again. The gas war, begun in 1940, will drag on for more than thirty years, leaving people and the land devastated. Then, in 1975 those living in the ruins of Everytown, in thrall to the local warlord, The Boss, see an unusual aircraft approaching. Small, streamlined, gleaming black and silver, with a curious wing, it lands nearby. As its pilot emerges, dressed in a shiny black pressure suit, it becomes clear that the Perspex bubble of the aircraft's cockpit forms an integral part of his spacesuit; man and machine are fused. This extra-

John Cabal approaches in a Hawker Fury. A still from *Things to Come* (1936).

ordinary streamlined design – the work of the Surrealist artist John Armstrong – is worn by the same John Cabal whom we met earlier, now the leader of a new order of airmen, 'Wings Over the World', an organization formed out of the remnant of the old engineers and mechanics, a 'brotherhood of efficiency, a free masonry of science'. The man whose fireplace was once adorned with a naïvely painted image of a Douglas DC-3 now stands as one of 'the last trustees of civilization', of 'law and sanity', of 'order and trade'.

A Style of Speed

At 7.20 p.m. on 10 July 1938, a specially modified Lockheed Lodestar taxied towards the main runway at Long Island's Floyd Bennett Field. A streamlined silver monoplane originally designed to carry twelve passengers on short trips across the US, the Lodestar was now heavily laden with the contingency supplies its pilot thought might be needed for a circumnavigation of

Cabal's return in 1975. A still from *Things to Come* (1936).

the globe –1,500 gallons of aviation fuel, 150 gallons of motor oil, countless spare parts, and several thousand ping-pong balls to make the aircraft buoyant if it were forced to ditch. At the controls was Howard Hughes, the celebrated industrialist and Hollywood mogul, whom *Life* would describe as 'a rich young Texan with a poet's face'; alongside him was the co-pilot, Harry Connor, and in the rear cabin sat a crew of three mechanics. After taking off they headed east, crossing the Atlantic via Newfoundland, and stopping first in Paris for refuelling. They then headed into Europe, where they were buzzed by Luftwaffe pilots over German airspace, before landing to a warm welcome in the Soviet Union. Taking a route across Siberia, and then travelling over the Bering Strait to Alaska, they arrived back at Floyd Bennett Field at 2.37 p.m. on 14 July. Hughes had made no unscheduled stops and had scarcely deviated from his plotted course, and his machine had covered 23,856 km (14,824 miles) in 3 days, 19 hours and 17 minutes – exactly half the previous

The Lockheed Lodestar in which Howard Hughes flew around the world in July 1938.

record; it would be nine years before anyone would circle the globe at greater speed.

At the time Lowell Thomas, the famous CBS radio journalist, exclaimed: 'The whole country is captivated by this heroic young man and how he has not let himself be spoiled by inherited wealth.'[11] More recent commentators have been less impressed by Hughes's exploit. Paul Virilio, for instance, suggests that the tycoon's only effort was 'to fake the speed of his destiny, to make his style of life a style of speed', in order to create 'an aesthetics of disappearance':

> This taste for ubiquitous absence he'll quench, first through his use of various technical media, in surpassing what was then the most presti-gious speed record: the 14th of July, 1938, his Lockheed-Cyclone having flown around the world 'in a great circular arc', lands at Floyd Bennett Field where he had taken off on July 10th. Then he guides his plane into the hangar to the exact point he left from.[12]

Virilio's error in identifying the Lodestone is revealing, since he clearly wants its Wright Cyclone engines to stand for the circular principle – rather than the magnetic attraction – of the whole enterprise; to reinforce the fact that this aircraft 'came back to the same spot'. This interpretation of Hughes's circumnavigation sug-gests that it achieved a near impossibility: its precision had ren-dered speed banal, shifting it out of the flight envelope of war-planes and into the world of the private aircraft; of lap-strapped luxury. Consequently Virilio dismisses Hughes as 'the Lindbergh of the end of the world', since after this 'his desire for movement is only desire of inertia, desire to see arrive what is left behind'.

These desires emerged first in the late 1920s when Hughes purchased a Boeing F4B-1, the Navy's new biplane fighter. He

thought it brilliantly manoeuvrable, but its top speed of 300 km/h (185 mph) was not fast enough, so he asked Douglas and later Lockheed to modify the airframe and engine to reduce drag and increase speed; the costs were of no consequence. In January 1934 Hughes entered the rebuilt fighter in the All-American Air Meet, flying it in the Sportsman-Pilots' Free-For-All. Over the four-lap race, covering 32 km (20 miles) with tight turns around pylons, his average velocity was close to the previous winner's top speed of almost 300 km/h (185 mph), and his margin of victory was so great that he almost lapped his nearest competitor. But even after his triumph, he demanded still more modifications for the Boeing, until it was suggested that it might be cheaper and easier to build his own plane, a machine that would become famous as the 'Silver Bullet'. By the time it was completed in August 1935, two years after work began on the project, Hughes had spent more than $120,000 on 'this beautiful little thing' and had created the world's most aerodynamically refined aircraft.

The machine was conceived by a recent graduate of the California Institute of Technology, Richard W. Palmer, who had already caused a stir with his advanced designs. Like most new

The H-1 'Silver Bullet', the custom-designed machine in which Hughes broke the world air speed record in 1935.

aircraft of the time, it was a low-wing cantilevered monoplane with an aluminium monocoque fuselage. Wind tunnel tests on models led to the construction of a short, wing with a sophisticated cross-sectional shape developed at NACA, a rounded tip and a pronounced taper. The fuselage was to be unusually slim for its length, with its largest diameter at the engine, which would be a reliable, air-cooled radial, the Pratt & Whitney Twin Wasp, generating 700 hp from fourteen cylinders arranged in two banks, one behind the other, to reduce drag. The radial engine was wrapped in a new bell-shaped cowling and sported a nozzle-like exhaust directed toward the rear to contribute extra thrust. Innovatively, its oil was cooled by air funnelled through small, efficient ducts on the front edges of the wings. On other aircraft, even a retracted undercarriage remained partly exposed, causing drag, but on the 'Silver Bullet' the landing-gear retracted completely into wheel wells in the bottom of the wing, sealed with flush-fitting doors. The stressed skin of the fuselage was riveted to the frame as normal, but rather than overlapping adjoining sheets of aluminium, the engineers butt-jointed them for the smoothest surface possible, and then skimmed off the head of each rivet so that not the slightest imperfection remained to disturb the flow of air. The wings were even smoother than the fuselage, since they were covered with oversized sheets of plywood that were then trimmed, shaved and sanded to a perfect contour. Finally, densely woven fabric, stretched over the plywood, then sealed, doped, painted and waxed, slickened the wing.

Hughes's goal was to shatter the world's speed record for land aircraft, then standing at 505 km/h (314 mph) and set in December 1934 by the French pilot Raymonde Delmotte in a Caudron C-460. The rules were simple: the American would have to make two upwind and two downwind passes over a three-kilometre course at less than 60 metres (200 ft) above the ground. Photoelectric timers would measure his speed. To break the old record, Hughes would have to beat Delmotte's mark on each of four passes, and his average would become the new speed record. On Friday 13 September 1935, Hughes took off and quickly made the regulation four passes over the course in Santa Ana, California; his speeds were 355, 339, 351 and 340 mph. He then made three passes more to be sure he had four that clearly eclipsed the old mark, and was about to climb and turn for an eighth when the 'Silver Bullet's engine died, dry of fuel. When Hughes tried to switch to the auxiliary tank, nothing happened, so he let the speeding, power-less plane climb until it was on the verge of a stall, and then turned into the wind to set up a crash landing in a ploughed beet field near the airstrip. Observers raced to the site, where they found the aircraft, its propeller bent and its glass-smooth surface scratched. Straddling the fuselage was Hughes, furiously scrib-bling figures in a notebook, trying to calculate his average speed. The 'Silver Bullet' had achieved 352.388 mph, a record that stood only until 1937, when the Messerschmitt 109, a German fighter then being blooded in the skies over Spain, took the prize.

Willy Messerschmitt's career as an aircraft engineer had began in 1914, when as a sixteen-year-old he had designed and built a glider under the direction of Friedrich Harth, one of Germany's pioneers of flight. Since then he had always sought to create light-weight, low-drag monoplanes that could move through the air as smoothly as possible; certainly, Messerschmitt's many critics claimed that he still believed he was designing a sailplane when he created the fast but fragile Bf 109, and especially its distinctive oblong, high-lift wing. This employed leading-edge slots for extra lift (an unprecedented device for a fighter) as well as slotted ailerons interconnected to the flaps, and meant that the Bf 109 could climb faster than any other machine, especially at higher altitudes. The philosophy of the aircraft's design was simple: the marriage of the smallest, lightest and most aerodynamically efficient airframe to the largest and most powerful engines that became available. 'The designer does not only see the aircraft that is flying today', he once said. 'No, he looks much further into the future. Long before an aircraft is finished, he knows how it could have been improved. Our work will never cease.'[13] The Bf 109 went through numerous revisions in the decade or so it was in production, but it was the machine prepared for the landplane speed record that best encapsulated its combination of power and finesse.

A new propeller and a more streamlined canopy were fitted; all slits on the fuselage were taped over, and the aluminium surface of the aircraft was highly polished. A specially prepared Daimler-Benz DB 6oi was shoehorned into the engine bay, capable of delivering no less than 1,700 hp when run with special sparking-plugs, manufactured by Bosch, and a heady cocktail of fuel. Since it had a very high compression, the engine could be run at full power for a short period only: it had to be warmed up with normal sparking-plugs, which then had to be replaced, all 24 of them, by the special plugs. Flying along the 3 km (1.86 miles) measuring stretch, which ran parallel to the track of the Augsburg–Buchloe railway, without an airspeed indicator and unable to use his flaps, Hermann Wurster, Messerschmitt's chief test pilot, achieved a mean speed of 610 km/h (379 mph), thereby bettering by nearly 50 km/h the previous record set by Hughes. Virilio suggested that Hughes's achievement was a question of 'the style of speed'; at the time of its announcement the Messerschmitt's record was much more substantial, since only a few weeks earlier, and to the consternation of many European air forces, the German Ministry of Propaganda had claimed that the Bf 109 now equipped all of the Luftwaffe's fighter units.[14]

A Messerschmitt Bf 109 being tested in the wind tunnel at the company's factory at
Adlershof, Bavaria, in 1938.

On 12 September 1931 the Supermarine S6B took part once more in the Schneider Trophy, awarded to the winner of an international race for floatplanes over a course of 150 nautical miles. There were no other competitors on this occasion and the machine, which had taken the prize two years earlier, now won again, at an average speed of 547 km/h (340 mph). It was the third British victory and secured the Trophy outright. Some months earlier, the Air Ministry, aware of the progress in aerodynamics that had been made by recent Schneider entries, had asked the nation's aircraft industry to provide some fresh designs for a single-seat day and night fighter that would have excellent manoeuvrability, a good range and, above all, exceptional speed, both in the climb to combat altitude and in straight and level flight. Of the eight designs submitted, five were biplanes, and after exhaustive trials in 1934, one of these, the Gloster Gladiator, won government approval and a large order from the RAF. Among the three monoplanes entered was the Supermarine Type 224, of which much was expected, if for no other reason than that it was created by Reginald Mitchell, the famous designer of the Schneider-winning floatplanes.

A pair of Supermarine S6s photographed prior to the 1931 Schneider Trophy event.

The opening scene of *The First of the Few*, Leslie Howard's film biography of Mitchell, shows the designer, in blazer and flannels, lying on Beachy Head gazing up through binoculars at the gulls wheeling overhead. He remarks to his wife, as she clears up their picnic, that the effectiveness of the birds' shape lay in its compact unity: 'Wings, body, tail, all in one. When we try, we build something all stuck together, with strings and struts and wires'. As he says this, he sketches, on the back of a works invitation, the outline of the machine that will win the Schneider trophy, and which would lead, thereafter, to the 224. This machine, known as a 'Spitfire', had an all-metal structure, a thick 'gull' wing from which sprouted a fixed undercarriage, enclosed in a streamlined fairing, and an open cockpit. The wings contained condensers for the steam-cooled Rolls-Royce Goshawk engine. It certainly looked fast and modern, and it was popular with its test pilots, yet in the trials Mitchell's Type 224 proved to be a design failure; the top speed was 228 mph, some 20 mph below estimates, and the climb to 15,000 ft took almost ten minutes, three and a half minutes longer than expected. The Gloster

Reginald Mitchell's sketch of the future form of aircraft. A still from *The First of the Few* (1942).

Gladiator could not only outclimb and out-turn this sleek mono-plane, but even outpace it.[15]

Immediately, Mitchell set about redesigning the 224. He short-ened and flattened the wings and fuselage, and installed an enclosed cockpit and retractable landing-gear to reduce drag. Though the aircraft, which Supermarine now called the Type 300, would thus gain about 30 mph in speed, it would still climb more slowly than the Type 224 because the wings were smaller. Then, in the autumn of 1934, Supermarine concluded an agreement with Rolls-Royce for a brand-new engine, the Merlin, named after the small but fierce European falcon or, as most engineers preferred, the Arthurian magician; in any event it would perform wonders on the Type 300. In static tests the Merlin showed it could generate nearly 800 hp – 140 hp more than the Goshawk in the Type 224 – and its developers saw few obstacles to increasing the output by another 25 per cent. With such power on tap, Mitchell calculated that his fighter could fly faster than 482 km/h (300 mph) and that its rate of climb would exceed the Gladiator's. The Air Ministry took notice and in April 1935 signed a contract with Supermarine

Mitchell's first attempt at a Spitfire: the Supermarine Type 224 at Hendon in 1934.

for an experimental fighter armed with six or eight machine-guns. The result, the Spitfire, would be regarded as one of the most thoroughbred of all planes: the aircraft that, in the opening sequence of Michael Powell and Emeric Pressburger's *A Canterbury Tale* (1944), emerges into the present from the shape of a merlin unleashed from a long dead pilgrim's hand; and which, in Monnington's *Southern England, 1944: Spitfires Attacking Flying Bombs*, seems to be perfectly in keeping with a pastoral scene drawn directly from Constable's *The Haywain*.

The first flight took place on 5 March 1936, witnessed by Mitchell, who was now in the terminal stages of cancer. Emerging from the hangar, the Spitfire – now painted a highly polished blue-grey, the finish of its fuselage shaving every joint and rivet – seemed the most elegantly proportioned aircraft ever produced. At his first encounter with 'the fastest machine in the world' at an air-

W. T. Monnington, *Southern England 1944: Spitfires Attacking Flying Bombs.*

field on the eve of the Battle of Britain, Richard Hillary was struck that the 'dull grey-brown of the camouflage could not conceal the clear-cut beauty, the wicked simplicity of the lines.'[16] Though bearing a passing resemblance to the smaller-spanned Messerschmitt Bf 109, the Spitfire's wings were elliptical. From the beginning it 'looked right'; indeed, it was so 'right' that 'Mutt' Summers, the test pilot, after landing from the first flight, told Mitchell, 'Don't touch anything'.[17] Another test pilot, Harald Penrose, later the author of the standard account of British aviation, recalled 'the rolling gait of the narrow undercarriage as I taxied out; the dropping wing and emphatic swing as the over-course fixed-pitch wooden propeller laboriously gripped the air, dragging the machine into a run faster and longer than anything I had experienced.'[18] The dying designer finally had the satisfaction of realizing that the magical figures for an advanced fighter, dreamt up in 1929 when he was designing the Schneider S6 to take the 2,000 hp Rolls-Royce R engine, had now been achieved, with a speed of 600 km/h (350 mph) and a climb to nearly 3,000 metres (10,000 ft) in three and a half minutes. Moreover, the embarrassment of the first version of the Spitfire could now be forgotten; indeed, as Penrose demonstrated, the new fighter was out for revenge:

> Suddenly a Gladiator appeared 1,000 ft above, its fixed cantilever undercarriage extended like an eagle's claws, offering the opportunity of a dog-fight. I drew the stick back in the manner I had become accustomed, forgetting the lightness of control. A vice clamped my temples, my face muscles sagged, and all was blackness. My pull on the stick relaxed instantly, but returning vision found the Spitfire almost vertical and the Gladiator a full 2,000 ft below.

Beyond the Barrier

A quiet afternoon over the White Cliffs of Dover, early in the war; the magazines have been emptied, and the blackened wreck of a Heinkel bomber lies strewn across the chalk downs: a raider on the shore. High above, a lone Spitfire performs a victory roll, its masked pilot dizzy with his machine's supple handling. On a whim, he puts his aircraft into a flat-out dive, gathering speed, 450, 500, 550 mph, and faster still until the machine begins to shake and those beautiful round-tipped wings, which have borne him up and away, now seem to be breaking away from the fuselage. Instinctively, he pulls back on the joystick to correct the descent, but the greater the force he exerts the further the Rolls-Royce-powered nose drops, until, desperate now, he throttles back and is able to pull out of the dive. He will later explain to his fellow pilots that it was as if he had 'suddenly run into a solid sheet of water, or something'. As the young Flying Officer holds the Spitfire on the straight and level again, a caption breaks into the frame, and announces the title of the film that has just begun: *The Sound Barrier.*

Later its director, David Lean, explained that the sequence prior to the credit was meant as an illustration, since it was possible that 'nobody would understand what the sound barrier was'.[19] Lean's film, financed by Alexander Korda and scripted by Terence Rattigan, himself an experienced airman, commences by depicting 'compressibility', that dramatic change in the way air behaves around the lifting surfaces of an aircraft as it approaches the speed of sound, and as the surrounding airflow itself becomes supersonic.[20] This phenomenon had puzzled pilots in the early 1940s, who would discover, often at the most inopportune moments with fighters on their tails, that their aircraft became temporarily

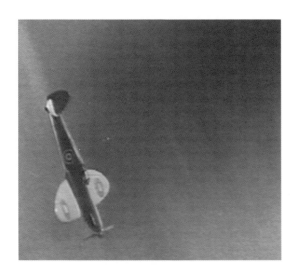

uncontrollable in steep dives, shaking and bucking as they approached the point at which the air reached sonic velocity, only to recover their usual handling characteristics at lower levels. Such phenomena seemingly defied explanation, but tests over the Californian desert in 1941 had provided a simple explanation: the speed of sound, and the associated effect, is higher in the warmer air at lower altitudes. As an aircraft dives, though its airspeed remains high, it is, in effect, retreating from the sound barrier, that 'great wall in the sky, strong enough to smash an aircraft into pieces', and beyond which, according to the widow of one of the test pilots depicted in Lean's film, is 'nothing, nothing at all'.[21]

Centring on John Ridgefield, the self-made owner of an aircraft manufacturing company, and his determination to construct a super-sonic aircraft, Rattigan's Academy Award-nominated script for *The Sound Barrier* considers the effect the quest for absolute speed has upon the will. Ridgefield's son Chris, whom he pushes to become a pilot (even though the young man is lacking in aeronautical

Spitfire in powered dive. A still from *The First of the Few* (1942).

aptitude), is determined to prove himself to his father. However, he dies on his first solo flight when his Gypsy Moth stalls and crashes short of the company airfield. Ridgefield's daughter, Susan, holds her father responsible for her brother's death and knows that his obsession to build the world's first supersonic jet will also result in the death of her husband: 'Is the ability to travel at 2,000 mph going to be a blessing to the human race?', she asks. Ridgefield replies smoothly that he could talk of 'beating the potential enemy bomber, or flying to New York in two hours', but the simple answer is that 'it's just got to be done'. His response is more evasive than that of his obvious original, Sir Geoffrey de Havilland, when excusing the death of one of his own test pilots:

> Why try and go faster? People ask. The answer is that in aviation, if you don't you are soon left far behind. Speed is the main advantage flying has to offer, and as long as people want to travel from place to place, they will want to do so as quickly as possible. This is one of the few invariable rules of human behaviour.[22]

At the end of *The Sound Barrier*, hailed by the American writer Tom Wolfe as 'one of the most engrossing films about flying ever made', and as 'supremely realistic', that 'great wall in the sky' is successful breached by the same British pilot we encountered diving the Spitfire over the Channel.[23] However, he now flies a silver machine named the Prometheus, an aircraft which in reality would in September 1953 break the World Absolute Air Speed Record, by flying at 1,184 km/h (735.72 mph) along the seafront at Tripoli, Libya, to prove itself emblematically, once and for all, as the Supermarine Swift. The aircraft was high-octane beauty; flawless, polished. Indeed the Prometheus steals *The Sound Barrier* from the film's wooden pilots; this is why Lean honours it in the opening

credits, along with the other aircraft featured in his film – the de Havilland Comet and Vampire, and the Supermarine Attacker – aircraft in a direct line of aerodynamic development that began little more than fifteen years earlier with the Spitfire. Just as the Spitfire had been the monument to Mitchell in the mid-1930s, so the Swift, the first British fighter to have sweep on the leading edges of wing and tail surfaces, would be the legacy of his brilliant but neglected successor, Joe Smith. When it appeared in 1948 the Swift was a fantastic machine, the most beautiful jet ever to emerge from a British aircraft factory; and Lean's film includes a montage depicting the various stages involved in the construction of the plane, one shot of which, taken from a gantry directly above the production line, makes the rear fuselage and tailfins resemble the base of a rocket on a launch pad, primed for lift-off. But the revolution was ubiquitous: the previous year the Americans had flown the all-swept wing F-86 Sabre, and in the Soviet Union, just a few months later, the similarly configured MiG-15 took to the sky for the first time, once more the fruits of German research on swept-wing aerodynamics

Generating speed: a Supermarine Spitfire Mk 22 flying in formation with a Supermarine Swift swept-wing jet fighter.

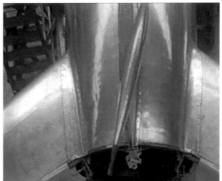

and high-speed flight. Within a couple of years, these machines would be dog-fighting it out over Korea, ducking and diving in ways even victorious Spitfire pilots could only dream about.

There was, however, yet another form of wing design that offered considerable advantages and, in some respects, would prove superior to the swept wing. In the early 1930s Alexander Lippisch, technical director of the Rhein glider company, had begun to explore the aerodynamic qualities of tailless aeroplanes and, in particular, the triangular wings he would term 'delta', after the shape of the fourth letter of the Greek alphabet. The delta had advantages denied to the purely swept wing – naturally, its swept leading edge and razor-thin section combined to delay the onset of compressibility, but in addition its great structural rigidity allowed space for engines, fuel and internal equipment. On his visit to the Messerschmitt factory in 1945, de Havilland's chief designer, Reginald Bishop, saw the material proof of Lippisch's concepts, the Me 163 'Komet'. It was effectively a glider: metal framed, wooden winged, fabric covered, and powered by a rocket that weighed only 165 kg (365 lb), yet developed a thrust of ten times that. Although the motor was flimsily attached to the airframe

The *Prometheus* – aka the Supermarine Swift – under construction. A still from *The Sound Barrier* (1951).

From above, the *empannage* of the *Prometheus* resembles the fins of a rocket. A still from *The Sound Barrier* (1951).

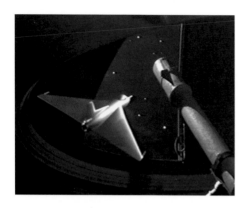

by just four bolts, its turbine was 'smaller than a margarine packet' and its regulator valve 'could easily be slipped into a trouser pocket', in 1941 an early version of this rocket machine, which was known by Luftwaffe pilots as the 'Devil's Sled', had flown at Mach 0.84, that is at 84 per cent of the speed of sound.[24] In reaction to this, Bishop constructed the DH.108 Swallow, a single-seat tail-less research aircraft built ostensibly to investigate the behaviour of delta wings, and to provide basic data for the Comet jet transport and the new Sea Vixen fighter. Design work began in October

The closing shot shows a model of a delta-wing jet, pointing the way to the stars. A still from *The Sound Barrier* (1951).

The Messerschmitt Me 163: the 'Devil's Sled'.

1945. De Havilland built three prototypes, the second of which, fitted with a boosted turbojet known as the Goblin, had the potential for supersonic flight. The aircraft flew for the first time at Hatfield in June 1946 and quickly attained true level speeds above the 991 km/h (616 mph) of the world's absolute speed record; its pilot was Geoffrey de Havilland, the son of the founder. On 27 September he took off from the firm's airstrip at Hatfield with the intention of making a high-speed practice flight over the Thames Estuary, involving a power dive from 3,000 metres (10,000 ft). Twenty minutes later eyewitnesses saw an aircraft break into several large pieces over the mudflats of Egypt Bay, north-east of Gravesend. Nearly all the wreckage was later recovered, including the engine, which examination showed not to have been at fault, and the subsequent enquiry established that the structure had failed under the very great loads experienced at air speeds in the region of Mach 0.9; but, as the pilot's father later recalled, 'Geoffrey's body was not found for several days, and then much further down the river.'[25]

In *The Sound Barrier*, Ridgefield's senior test pilot, played by Nigel Patrick, while driving home from the airfield with his wife, buys a newspaper. He notices the headline, 'JET PLANE EXPLODES: Geoffrey de Havilland killed FASTER THAN SOUND', and hides the

Crashes involving the de Havilland 108 'Swallow' would kill three of Britain's top test pilots.

paper from her; it contains a premonition of his own death. Both of the remaining Swallows crashed with fatal consequences just before Lean began shooting his film, but not before one of the aircraft had propelled a British pilot beyond Mach 1 for the first time. On 9 September 1948, John Derry, de Havilland's chief test pilot since the death of the founder's son, and one of the film's stunt pilots, exceeded the speed of sound in a power dive. The actress Ann Todd later recalled that he had a 'religious aura' to him; 'when he came into a room, everything lit up'.[26] Four years later, lighting up the skies in a DH.110 Sea Vixen fighter at the Farnborough Air Show, as he came down in a steep dive turn, generating the expected sonic boom for the crowds below, one of the wings failed. The constructor of the aircraft coolly recalled: 'It had presumably been overstrained previously. A complete break-up followed and the two jet engines were hurled into the crowded spectators, killing twenty-eight people. Derry and his observer, Tony Richards, were killed in a few seconds.'[27] De Havilland's 'presumably' bears the coolness of an accident investigator, while his 'few' carries the precision of the aircraft engineer. In the crowd that day were David Lean and his wife, Ann Todd. He later recalled that Derry's wife was

'Faster than Sound?' The death of de Havilland is announced. A still from *The Sound Barrier* (1951).

in the grandstand: 'So great was her shock . . . that she sat there as if nothing had happened. Another pilot had to come and take her away.'[28]

When Lean's film was shown in America it was retitled *Breaking Through the Sound Barrier*, much to the annoyance of the director. Attending the premiere was a USAF officer, who, though praising Lean's film as 'a good and very realistic action picture', had to put the record straight, all the same:

> They used a World War II Spitfire to break the barrier, which was amusing because that airplane wouldn't go faster than .75 Mach in a power dive. When the actor discovered that his stick froze at Mach 1, instead of pulling back, he pushed the stick forward and it somehow released. Any pilot who really tried that stunt would've drilled himself into the ground.

Worse was to follow after the film ended:

> When the lights came on, I realized that people seated around me thought they had watched a true story. I overheard one guy say to his wife, 'Where in hell was Uncle Sam?' I said to him, 'Hey, that was only a movie. We broke the barrier, not the damned British. And I'm the guy who did it.'[29]

Captain Charles E. 'Chuck' Yeager 'did it' in mid-October 1947, when his bright orange Bell X-1, named *Glamorous Glennis* in honour of his wife, dropped from the B-29 Superfortress parent ship at 35,000 feet, opened up its rockets and zoomed upward toward thinner air at just over 70,000 feet, making him the first pilot in history to fly faster than the speed of sound.

Development of his remarkable little plane had begun in 1943, an interesting cooperative enterprise combining NACA, the US

aerospace industry and the armed services. The initial impetus
came from NACA aerodynamicist, John Stack, and Bell Aircraft
Corporation engineer Robert J. Woods, who both felt that pro-
peller-driven planes had nearly reached the limits of high-speed
performance, and so began work on a research plane to probe
transonic and supersonic flight characteristics. Jet engines
under development at the time in the US fell far short of the
required thrust, so designers constructed the plane around a
rocket engine supplied by a firm named Reaction Motors,
Incorporated, and which combusted a mixture of alcohol and
distilled water along with liquid oxygen to produce a thrust of
6,000 pounds. Hence Tom Wolfe described the X-1 as 'a fat
orange swallow with white markings. But it was really just a
length of pipe with four rocket chambers in it.'[30] When the liquid

The Bell X-1 experimental aircraft in 1949.

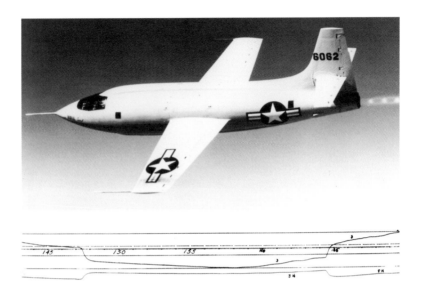

oxygen rolled out of the hoses and into the belly of the X-1 it started boiling off, and gave the impression that the little machine was fuming. When Yeager, played by Sam Shepherd, first catches sight of it in Philip Kaufman's film version of *The Right Stuff*, he's out on an early morning ride; hot and bulbous, it looks like a smoking revolver, just dropped to the desert floor.

The engine was one of the few weird aspects of the X-1. Not much was known about the flight speeds for which the plane was intended, though there was much compelling aerodynamic data available for the .50-calibre machine-gun bullet, the speed of which the X-1 was intended to exceed; hence, its fuselage shape was keyed to this ballistic information. The thin, conventionally straight wings – only 90 mm (3$^{1}/_{2}$ inches) – were stressed for eighteen times the plane's weight to compensate for extreme loads anticipated at sonic speeds. Since the engine's fuel lasted only

The Bell X-1 in flight in 1947, with a copy of the paper-tape record of the world's first supersonic flight, or 'mach jump', which took place that year.

about two and a half minutes, the X-1 was designed to be launched like a bomb from a B-29 parent ship. During 1946 Bell's test pilots flew unpowered drops to check out release systems and 'dead-stick' landings, followed by preliminary powered flights. Then Yeager took over for eight special flights, increasing speeds and altitudes in preparation for the milestone mission, which he flew despite being incapacitated by two broken ribs sustained in a fall from his horse on the eve of the mission. By this time, he was confident that he had mastered 'the orange beast'; that *Glamorous Glennis* would never play any 'dirty tricks' without fair warning. So it would prove. After the aircraft exceeded Mach 1, and the sonic boom thundered out over the desert, Yeager experienced a sense of anti-climax, he later expressed in his own terms: 'The Ughknown was a poke through Jello. Later on, I realized that this mission had to end in a let-down, because the real barrier wasn't in the sky, but in our knowledge and experience of supersonic flight.'[31]

Almost as soon as the barrier was breached, engineers began to expand the envelope of flight. Conventional aerodynamics had emphasized the importance of the wing, above and beyond the rest of the aircraft; the fuselage had always been considered a structural necessity, the best place for a pilot. Now, it would assume equal importance, as it and the wings came to be considered a blended whole, in what was known as the 'area rule'. As new designs were assayed to minimize the disturbance of the air as it flowed around the body of the aircraft, engineers reduced the diameter of the fuselage to create a wasp-waist, drawn in where the wings were attached. The Convair F-102, a scalpel-edged delta wing, which to the surprise of its engineers barely made Mach 1, was redesigned according to the 'rule' with a longer fuselage, incorporating a tapered midbody section and a larger tailfin. With other minor changes the redesigned aircraft took to the air

in December 1954, achieving Mach 1.25 with ease on its second flight.

The F-102A was the first of a successful line of tailless delta-winged aircraft, known as the 'Century Series', which reached its zenith with the F-104 'Starfighter'. This flew for the first time in 1954. Radical in design, it consisted of a small, slender fuselage containing a single afterburning Wright turbojet, and supporting two tiny razor wings and a large vertical fin surmounted by a high-set tailplane. The first combat aircraft capable of sustained flight at Mach 2, it could *climb* at speeds in excess of Mach 1, its form leading the poet J. H. Prynne to describe how its 'Exhaust washes tidal flux / at the crust, the fierce acceleration of mawkish regard'.[32] In fact the faster it flew, the less 'mawkish' its pilot would become; at low speeds it was unstable with an ugly

The century series of US jet fighters in perfect formation. Clockwise, from top: the McDonnell F-101 Voodoo; the Convair F-102 Delta Dagger; the North American F-100 Super Sabre; the Lockheed F-104 Starfighter.

tendency to pitch up and flame out its engine, before snapping into rolls and spins, to fall, as Tom Wolfe puts it, 'like a length of pipe' or 'a set of car keys'.[33]

Yet despite its inherent aerodynamic instability, in 1963 Lockheed produced a special version of the jet for NASA, the NF-104, which was a Starfighter with a rocket engine motor over the tailpipe, using hydrogen peroxide and JP4 fuel to deliver an extra 2,700 kg (6,000 lb) of thrust where it was needed most: a quarter of the way to space. Its designers confidently assumed that the main engine combined with the regular afterburner would take the jet to about 60,000 ft, at which point the rocket would cut in, and propel it somewhere between 120,000 and 140,000 ft. Hence, NASA trainee astronauts would don silver pressure suits, and take this idealized version of the Starfighter up in a massive parabolic flight, which would afford up to two minutes of weightlessness, during which

The Starfighter, a fighter-interceptor built to counter the MiG-21, could climb at speeds in excess of Mach 1 and could achieve Mach 2.2 on the level.

time they could master the use of the 'reaction controls', hydrogen-peroxide thrusters of the sort used above 100,000 feet in all experimental craft, such as the North American X-15. However, the engineers were uncertain how the NF-104 would handle in thin air above this altitude; the limits of its performance envelope were unknown. Chuck Yeager, however, seized the opportunity to test it and attempt a new altitude record for an aircraft taking off under its own power, a record currently standing at 113,890 ft, set in 1961 by a Russian pilot flying the E-66A, a delta-winged fighter.

Having taken the Lockheed up for three checkout flights, pushing it up gradually toward 100,000 ft, where the limits of the envelope, whatever they were, would begin to reveal themselves, Yeager went out for a last preliminary flight before the record attempt the following day. It was a gorgeous December afternoon, and he accelerated, as before, from 40,000 ft, coming over the top of the arc at 104,000 ft. But as the machine's angle of attack reached 28 degrees, its short, mean wings blanketed its T-shaped tail, causing the nose suddenly to rise dramatically. Unable to control it with the peroxide thrusters, Yeager later recalled 'the damned airplane finally fell off flat, and went into a spin . . . like a record on a turntable'. The flight data recorder would later indicate that before it made impact with the desert floor the Starfighter made fourteen revolutions; Yeager sat tight through thirteen of them, before reluctantly ejecting: 'I hated losing an expensive airplane, but I couldn't think of anything else to do.'[34] Though only lightly injured, Yeager never again attempted to set a record, to fight through to the stars in the desert sky.

Speedbirds

In the late 1950s, the French critic Roland Barthes claimed that what strikes one first about the pressure-suited jet-man – a pilot such as a Geoffrey de Havilland, a John Derry or a Chuck Yeager – was the simple fact that his work involved the elimination of speed; the fact that 'an excess of speed turns into repose', that luxury of velocity that Virilio had identified in Howard Hughes. Just before the flight in which his plane disintegrated Geoffrey de Havilland described the experience of high-speed jet flight: 'so smooth, it was like driving a quiet car off into the sky. I found myself tapping instruments to make sure the needles weren't sticking.'[35] Whereas the pilot-heroes such as Saint-Exupéry, or even Lindbergh (who, as Barthes is keen to remind us, 'flew in a lounge-suit'), had been made unique by a whole sense of speed as experience, of space consumed, of intoxicating motion, the jet-man, by contrast, is defined by a 'coenaesthesis of motionless . . . as if the extravagance of his vocation precisely consisted in *over-taking* motion, in going faster than speed.'[36]

It takes quite a machine to achieve such a state of technological sublimity, not least because of practical constraints. On aircraft capable of supersonic speeds for brief periods only, structural problems are relatively minor, as there is insufficient time for the heat generated on the outer skin to permeate into the airframe. On prolonged supersonic flights, however, the situation alters radically, as the temperatures generated can rise to a level where the entire structure begins to fail. During the late 1950s, as NASA began preparations for space exploration, a number of very high-speed flights were made by the rocket-powered North American X-15, designed to fly more than 50 miles high. On 3 October 1967, after setting a number of amazing records, the X-15A-2, flown by Major William 'Pete' Knight, pushed the record to Mach 6.72 – the fastest speed ever achieved by a powered aircraft. Such achievements led directly to the NASA Space Shuttle, a powered spacecraft that becomes an un-powered glider when it re-enters

the Earth's atmosphere at blinding speed – Mach 24 – where the air friction on its underside builds to over 3,000°F, at which point it becomes the world's fastest and most structurally advanced aircraft, owing its survival to hundreds of thousands of ceramic tiles placed over its fuselage. However, the loss of the *Columbia* in February 2003, breaking up 40 miles above eastern Texas, shows that even that novel and expensive solution could not always overcome fundamental aerodynamic issues.

An early solution for prolonged supersonic flight was to use the aircraft itself as a 'heat-soak', high skin heat being absorbed or soaked away, and dangerous peaks in load-carrying members prevented by sophisticated composite materials, spun off from space research. One of the first aircraft designed to 'soak' in supersonic conditions was the curiously named fighter-bomber,

The rocket powered X-15, built by North American, flew at six times the speed of sound, and reached heights only to be exceeded by manned spacecraft.

the Convair B-58 'Hustler'. This aircraft could exceed the speed of sound for more than two hours continuously and had a maximum speed of approximately twice the speed of sound. At such speeds, parts of its skin were heated to over 1,200°C by a combination of air friction, the proximity of jet exhausts from the four after-burning engines, and by heat from the massive electronic systems on board. In order to provide the required strength and rigidity, large portions of the B-58 were fabricated from brazed stainless-steel honeycomb sandwich panels, consisting of a core, first fabricated from strips of thin stainless-steel, brazed together, then machined, and finally placed between re-formed inner and outer skins. When complete the panel was relatively light, extremely rigid, and retained its strength up to a temperature of 1,260°C. The expense was, however, extremely high; the airframe of the B-58 literally cost more than its weight in gold, although it soon became clear that its active service life was destined to be rather short. Even its extraordinary performance could no longer guarantee success against increasingly sophisticated Soviet surface-to-air missiles.

The Convair B-58 Hustler, the world's first supersonic bomber, saw limited deployment owing to its inherent fragility.

Nevertheless, the USAF decided to publicize the capabilities of its new B-58s to capture a series of aviation records. On 10 May 1961 a Hustler flew a 1,073-kilometre closed course in half an hour to win the prize, established by Louis Blériot back in 1930, to be awarded to any aircraft flying for at least 30 minutes at an average speed of 2,000 km/h. Just over a fortnight later another Hustler, en route to the 1961 Paris Air Show, set a New York–Paris speed record, covering the route in 3 hours 20 minutes at an average speed of 1,742 km/h (1,089.36 mph). New records were set on 5 March 1962, when a Hustler flew non-stop on a round trip from Los Angeles to New York, the first leg (Los Angeles–New York) taking 2 hours (averaging 1,955 km/h or 1,214 mph) and the return being completed in 2 hours 15 minutes, at an average speed of 1,739 km/h (1,081 mph). This was the first transcontinental flight in history in which the vehicle moved across the country faster than the rotational speed of the earth. Six months later a B-58 flew from Tokyo to London, and spent five hours solidly supersonic; this flight alone set five world absolute records. And yet, despite such immense speed, and the esteem its delta shape brought to the designers at Convair's plant at Fort Worth, the Hustler quickly developed a reputation for its dirty tricks. Almost a quarter of the 116 aircraft built were destroyed in accidents before the type was removed from service in 1968, and, in addition, several other Hustlers were damaged seriously enough to prevent them from being returned to flight status. Some of the accidents were due to pilot error, but most were a result of mechanical or systems failures that were often a consequence of the B-58's quantum leap in technology.

Its successor, the North American B-70 Valkyrie, was conceived in 1959. In the same year that the Air Force had taken delivery of its first Mach 2 interceptor – the Starfighter – it was seriously proposed that a nuclear bomber be built with a take-off

weight of more than 244 tonnes (538,000 lb), and a top speed *three* times that of sound. The suggestion came from research published three years earlier, in March 1956, when NACA scientists encountered a phenomenon called compression lift, which had emerged from computer models of a bullet-like shape being propelled at supersonic speed and surrounded by a high-pressure shock cone. The aero-dynamicists suggested attaching wings to the bullet, so dividing into two the very shock cone, and then, as it were, removing the top half of the bullet. The corresponding shape left under the wing created a compression wave that pushed it up; the net result, in the calculations, at least, was indistinguishable from lift in more conventional supersonic wing forms, but without the concomitant, heat-inducing drag.

The XB-70, a research aircraft derived from the B-70 supersonic bomber.

Over the next five years, engineers at North American worked to create a massive machine along the lines suggested by the NACA team, an aircraft which, like no other, would combine the inorganic forms of supersonic aerodynamics with the sheer presence of a killer. When it was rolled out of its hangar in 1964, the prototype of the Valkyrie looked as if it had emerged from another atmosphere, the combination of its long, narrow undulating fuselage, its square forward 'canard' elevators, and its cockpit visor rendering the aircraft reptilian, cobraic. But that impression faded into awe as the gently curled leading edges of the huge delta wings came into view, hinged at the outer sections so as to fold downward, first to 25, and then to 60 degrees as speed increased. The folded tips behaved as ventral fins, aiding lateral directional stability and reducing the need for larger, heavy vertical fins, while vortices at the wing tip were forced beneath the aircraft and trapped, so that the B-70 could be said to 'surf' on its own shock wave, a style of flight that perhaps led to its Wagnerian name.[37]

However, the B-70 had met its nemesis even before its first flight, made on 21 September 1964. During the presidential campaign of 1960, Kennedy had criticized the Eisenhower administration's defence cut-backs, but once he became President, he too had little time for the technological extravagance of the defence programme. Consequently, in March 1961, following the downing of Gary Powers's high-performance U-2 over western Russia, Kennedy announced that the B-70 would only perform research into high-speed flight. The ballistic missile, not the manned supersonic bomber, had become the keystone of US defence policy, and Kennedy's Secretary of Defense, Robert McNamara, made clear his belief that a better strategic method might consist of a small aircraft overflying the enemy to direct an ICBM to its target.

The Lockheed SR-71 Blackbird was built for reconnaissance at very high altitudes and speeds.

The machine McNamara had in mind for this role was the Lockheed SR-71 – the Blackbird – and it emerged out of paranoia. Despite the fact that surface-to-air missiles now spelled the end of overflights of the USSR by U-2s, the 'deep-penetration' mission was still vital. To survive Soviet fighters and air defences, in addition to high altitude, vast speed and radar stealth were now required, and these demands advanced the technology of the time. The airframe needed to be able to soak at high temperatures for long periods of supersonic flight, and other requirements included a low-drag wing, able to provide sufficient lift in the attenuated air at operational altitudes, and a low radar cross-section to delay detection. The Blackbird met all these demands. First flown in December 1964, it could conceivably reach Mach 3.4 (making it the fastest aeroplane ever to enter 'front-line' service), sustain flight at 26,000 m (85,000 ft), and exceed 27,700 km (17,250 miles) with in-flight refuelling. It also had the ability to scan more than 100,000 square miles of the Earth's surface per hour from above 80,000 ft.

The aircraft had the form of a large tailless delta wing, with the turbo-ramjets mounted outboard to avoid the worst of the shock wave from the nose at trisonic speeds; the head of the CIA, who had commissioned the Blackbird, described these engines as 'the hammers of hell'. Twin fins sprouting from the rear of the engine nacelles were pushed inwards, partly for aerodynamic reasons and partly to create a stealthy radar signature. Wing-body blending, coupled with a subtle fin running the entire length of the forward 'fuselage', also helped to reduce the aircraft's electronic visibility. Beneath the black 'iron ball', radar-absorbing paint finish, most of the structure was made of titanium, at the time an exotic, untried material, but one able to withstand the kinetic heating of flight at Mach 3. As it happened, much of the less classified aerodynamic data derived from the Blackbird was channelled into a NASA

programme to consider the feasibility of a Mach 3 supersonic transport, or SST; and here it joined that derived from the two XB-70 airframes, still flying for the sake of research. However, the entire programme was set back in 1966 when, during a formation photo shoot, the second XB-70, its airframe now incorporating improvements suggested during flight tests of the first aircraft, and heavily laden with in-flight computers, collided, ironically enough, with one of the F-104 Starfighters escorting it.

Nevertheless, later that year, after approximately eight years of research and analysis, a Boeing design for the SST was selected. It was not until December 1969, however, three years later, that President Nixon gave the final stamp of approval to the US supersonic transport development programme, making available funds

The Boeing Supersonic Transport (SST) undergoing windtunnel tests at NASA's Langley facility in 1966.

for the start of construction of a prototype. Its appearance was described in a Boeing prospectus:

> a long, sleek, aerodynamically clean airplane with a slender fuselage, swept delta wing, and conventional tail. Power is supplied by four General Electric GE4 turbojet engines mounted in individual pods at the trailing edge of the wing. It will be built entirely of titanium, . . . and fully capable of the heat generated by flight at almost three times the speed of sound.[38]

This sounds familiar enough now as a rough outline of the style, if not the substance, of those supersonic passenger aircraft – the Concorde and the Tupolev Tu 144 – then under development in Europe. However, there is a 'BIG difference between the American SST and the Russian and British/French supersonic', the Boeing pamphlet exclaims: 'the foreign designs are built of aluminium with respective speeds of 1500 and 1400 mph [Mach 2 and 2.2]. The Boeing 2707-300 will fly at 1800 mph [Mach 3]!'

As it happened, environmental experiments carried out by the Valkyrie team had already caused the SST programme to disintegrate; supersonic flight by airliners, no matter how high they flew, would have too great a sonic boom at ground level to ever be acceptable, and in March 1971 Congress voted to cancel the entire programme. For Paul Virilio, however, the issue behind the discontinuation was not noise pollution. Rather, the SST 'wasn't built because the Americans were very worried at the idea of building a civilian supersonic jet that would go faster than military jets'; such a state of affairs would prove that now speed was tending towards civil luxury rather than military need.[39] Certainly, that is how it seemed to a group of USAF pilots recalled by Jock Lowe, British Airways' longest-serving Concorde pilot:

The success of Concorde was first really illustrated to me the first time I flew to an airshow at Toronto, where we met some SR-71 Blackbird spy-plane pilots, and they said that they had been used to flying photographic missions at 60,000 feet over Cuba for many years in their spacesuits and bonedomes. One day air traffic control asked them to move 20 miles to the right and they asked why. Control said 'Because you have an aircraft coming past you, coming out from Caracas', and they said 'and there we were looking, and there was an Air France Concorde which went past us with a hundred people sitting in shirt-sleeves drinking champagne'. And they sat there in their spacesuits.[40]

4 Model Planes

Intellectual Things

In the opening sequence of David Cronenberg's 1997 film version of J. G. Ballard's *Crash*, Catherine (Deborah Unger), a tall blonde woman – 'a luxurious mannequin, a Dali doll' – in a black silk blouse, is taken by the planes in the darkened hangar; by the smooth expanses of the Beechcraft's fuselage, by the struts and floats of the Grumman Goose flying boat, by the tapering cheat-lined nose and the wing-mounted engines of the Cessna 501, in which the 'tired executives might sigh relief'.[1] Another, smaller Cessna looks away as, aroused by the closeness of these aircraft, Catherine unbuttons her blouse, opens the cup of her bra and places the nipple of her right breast against the nacelle of the star-board engine of the 501; light aircraft and heavy petting. A moment later, a man approaches – a flying instructor, in fact – and, manoeuvring her against the flaps of the aircraft, enters her from behind; she barely moves, but stands bent, her skirt raised, as the camera continues on its tracking shot through the echoing hangar, that 'mansion of machine' W. H. Auden once described as being so 'motherly to metal'.[2]

From a brief hint in Ballard's novel, Cronenberg's film has arrived at a familiar topos of the hangar, the aircraft park, as a

Stills from the opening sequence of David Cronenberg's controversial adaptation of J. G. Ballard's *Crash*.

place in which dreams and fantasies can be modelled and enacted, safely and irresponsibly, and rendered it sexually explicit. In *The Mint*, T. E. Lawrence's account of his life as Aircraftsman Ross, the pseudonym he assumed to join the RAF after his nervous breakdown, the hangar becomes the centre of his world: 'its girders sheathed in iron, creating an open space, without one pillar or obstruction across its main expanse . . . as great as most cathedrals'. As the light fades, it becomes a space as transformative for him as it is for Catherine Ballard:

> At night it looks a palace. We switch on lamp after lamp, high in the roof, and a wedge of golden light pours through the open front across the illimitable aerodrome which runs up, saucer-like, to a horizon like the sea, and sea-coloured, of waving grey-green grass. In this stream of light puny figures, eight or ten of them, swim, at a game of push and pull around the glitter-winged Bristol Fighters or Nine Acks. They drag them one by one into the lighted cave: then the doors clang shut, the lights go out: and the dwarfs trickle out from a dwarf-door in rear, across grass and gravel, bedwards.[3]

Here is the magic of the place; the aircraft themselves, khaki and canvassed, the staples of the RAF in the years immediately after the Great War, become precious objects, to be removed back into the cave by tiny helpers who minister to their every need. These are machines that diminish those around them; and diminish their ability to come to terms with them.

In an article for *Vogue* in March 1942, Paul Nash reviewed the war work he had undertaken during his brief appointment as official artist by the Air Ministry two years earlier. He claimed that, notwithstanding the approach from the authorities, his fresh interest in war art had emerged from his realization that in the current

conflict, 'machines were the real protagonists'; and that, despite the vast human forces involved in their support, the fact that the tasks of military personnel were directed mechanically meant that pictorially, at least, individuals had been rendered insignificant, in contradistinction to the 'personality' of those machines they employed as weapons.[4] At first glance, this might be an attempt to justify the notorious desertion of his war art, but as his essay continues, it becomes clear that Nash's preoccupation with the way aircraft 'look' contains larger issues which are pertinent to the relationship between aesthetics and technology.

Despite his repeated requests, the RAF refused to take Nash up, even in one of its most unsophisticated training aircraft; he had been suffering from 'cardiac asthma' since the First World War, and it was feared he might lose consciousness even at low altitudes. Undaunted at being left on the ground, he began his Air Ministry commission by becoming a 'plane-spotter'. He subscribed to *Flight* and *The Aeroplane*, filling the walls of his rooms with images, courtesy of the Photograph Division at the Ministry of Information,

A photograph by Paul Nash of a Vickers Wellington being 'bombed up', 1940. The type was the mainstay of RAF Bomber Command in the early days of the war.

of those aircraft he might encounter at RAF airfields in the vicinity of Oxford, where he was then living; 'changing the prints from time to time and gaining gradually, I thought, through their constant presence, a sense of their essential nature and behaviour.' Then, having visited the men, and photographed the machines at the many local Bomber Command bases, he pasted these prints into folders, poring over them, like a professional model-maker, before assembling an equivalent image in watercolour on the opposite page. Denied the opportunity to experience these unfamiliar models in their own element, it was as if he needed to rivet them in his material sense before he set to work on them with his imagination; yet in the final analysis, it was only when he had absented himself from these insistent factual details – the structural idiosyncrasies that all aircraft exhibit – that he could project them into works of art. It is not too fanciful to suggest that prior to making that 'free, rough drawing in line, generally upon a dark paper which would "take" both a hard wax chalk and water colour in thin washes', Nash was behaving as an enthusiast removing model aircraft from their stands and, taking them in hand, imagining 'the fighter tearing across the spaces of the sky and the bomber ploughing through the clouds', towards, say the target area over Berlin, or the barges at Le Havre.

'The Personality of Planes' essay was intended to provide *Vogue*'s readers with an imaginative retrospective of the aircraft that Nash felt most at home with during Britain's 'darkest hour': the Armstrong-Whitworth Whitley, the Handley-Page Hampden, the Vickers Wellington and the Bristol Blenheim, together forming the spine of the nation's skeletal bomber force at the outbreak of war. An earlier essay, 'Bomber's Lair', written in 1940, had acted as the prototype in this respect, Nash recalling his passing an Air Force Station at twilight, just as a gathering storm 'cast over the lower sky a dark wing of gloom'. From the road skirting the aerodrome, it was possible to divine only 'the vague structure of certain mechanical creatures winged and finned indoors. Out in the great field between the hangars and the road a number of others stretched their great bellies, pointed wings stiffly outspread, and huge tail fins proudly erected.'[5] In the later essay, Nash would identify these aircraft and give them painterly distinction.

Take his treatment of the Whitley. Designed as a troop carrier in 1932, and then reworked as a bomber, it was the first British bomber type over Germany; on the first night of the war, a large force of them flew across the North Sea to Hamburg, Bremen and the Ruhr, and dropped six million leaflets in an attempt to convince the German people that war was avoidable. Six months later, on 19 March 1940, a Whitley made the first bombing raid on enemy soil. The aircraft always flew in a characteristic 'nose-down' attitude, its wing design less than ideal. In Nash's view, such an aircraft, 'in form very long, very narrow, with a wide wingspan and well-balanced tail features', 'a body, elongated and rigid', and a 'depressed' nose was, 'as Blake said of a tear, . . . an intellectual thing'.[6] Nash has in mind lines addressed to the Deists in Blake's *Jerusalem*:

> For a Tear is an Intellectual thing;
> And a Sigh is the Sword of an Angel King
> And the bitter groan of a Martyrs woe
> Is an Arrow from the Almighties bow.[7]

Certainly, the slow and vulnerable Whitley produced its fair share of tears, sighs, and 'bitter groans' among its flight crews before it was withdrawn from front-line service early in 1942.

Accompanying the Whitleys on the first attack on Germany was the strangest of Nash's aerial creatures, the Handley-Page Hampden.

He is the first to admit that 'The lineaments of its design are not very prepossessing. It lacks the symmetry of some planes I have described; it is rather clumsy . . . We can only find the equivalent of the Hampden bomber in the mists of prehistory. It is plainly some sort of pterodactyl.'[8] This flying dinosaur of Bomber Command had entered service only in 1938 and performed without distinction, suffering particularly heavy losses in daylight raids, owing to its inadequate defensive armament, which consisted of only five 0.303 inch machine-guns, the positioning of which left numerous blind spots. Unaware of the irony of his description, Nash continues by claiming that he loves the aircraft 'because it is a devil. It sets out across the darkling fields soaring into the dusk with its great satanic nose snuffing the upper air.' Certainly, among the pilots who had flown it, the Hampden had a diabolical reputation. Of all-metal construction, the fuselage had a distinctive deep fore-body housing the crew of four, and a relatively slender tail-boom carrying the tailplane and twin fins and rudders, a configuration leading to its nickname, the Flying Suitcase. This, however, was not affectionately applied: cramped accommodation led to fatigue on long flights, and in an emergency it was almost impossible for members of the crew to gain access to each other's stations.[9]

In the earlier essay, Nash recalled how shortly after starting 'to make records for the Air Ministry', he found himself alone inside a hangar housing Vickers Wellington bombers, which immediately struck him as 'huge mammalian carcases . . . with their great heads and erect fin tails', and brought back the thrill he felt in the 'alarming departments of the Natural History Museum at South Kensington where fish gradually cease and mammals begin and great sharks give place to small whales until all about one are the mighty whales'.[10] As in T. E. Lawrence's account, the light in the hangar is 'eccentric' and casts 'exaggerated shadows and silhouettes

from the conspicuous parts of the bombers, their fins and the "fly-ing eggs" of the aerials'. Presently an aircraftsman approaches the Wellington, and Nash engages him in a discussion about 'the nature of airplanes', suggesting that it was wrong to compare them to birds: '"Birds", [the aircraftsman] said, with indignant emphasis, "I always think my old girl looks like a ruddy whale."'

In *Hamlet,* the Prince tries to make Polonius agree about the nature of a cloud that may be passing overhead: it is like a camel, a weasel, or a whale: 'Yes, very like a whale', says the old courtier to the young man, humouringly.[11] The indignant humour of the aircraftsman is carried into this later essay: the Wellington 'resembles the whale so nearly that there seems no reason why it should not start spouting in the sky at any moment. To watch the dark silhouette of a Wellington riding the evening clouds is to

Paul Nash, *Wellington Bomber Watching the Skies* (1940).

see almost the exact image of the great killer whale hunting in unknown seas.' Such a cetacean aspect clearly emerges in, *Wellington Bomber Watching the Skies*; the great form broods in its hangar, its snout pointing at a strip of sky, waiting to emerge into its element. By time Nash was writing this in 1942, however, the Wellington, the long-range night bomber waiting, like Polonius's daughter, for darkness to fall, was almost universally regarded by the air-crew who flew and serviced it not as a whale, but instead as the 'Wimpy', in honour of J. Wellington Wimpy, the well-rounded gourmet of the Popeye cartoons, who would 'gladly pay you Tuesday for a hamburger today'.[12] Perhaps this is why, when describing the aircraft two years later, Nash seeks to tone down his account: 'Even so the Wellington is not a whale.' In fact, it seems that the aircraft is a victim of its own success, since it has become 'boringly popular', getting 'all the searchlight as it were', mainly, he suggests, because it is 'very human in one way. It is jolly, it is on the plump side, I see that now.'

Bristol Blenheim under attack. A still from *The Way to the Stars* (1944).

The final, and most satisfying, account of an Aerial Creature concerns the Bristol Blenheim, the versatile and swift fighter-bomber that entered service in 1937 but which features rather sorrily in *The Way to the Stars* (1945), to suggest something of the desperate failure of Bomber Command's daylight operations during the first years of the war. Before he takes off, the inexperienced Pilot Officer Penrose (John Mills) is warned by the aptly named Corporal Fitter (Charles Victor) that the aircraft's engines are a 'bit overdue for a major' service, but that given the shortages, the machine cannot be freed up. He adds darkly: 'It's a wicked shame to treat aircraft like this, sir. No good will come of it.' Clearly, by the time he came to describe the Blenheim, Nash too had realized that his own treatment of this machine – which was produced in two variants, the Short or Long Nose – needed overhauling, in the direction of the human form: 'the short-nose Blenheim is, naturally, enigmatical. You might say it has no face – which is true, in a sense, and also terrifying – but I would prefer to say it wears a mask, or that behind a mask it is growing a face which, when at last it appears, may eclipse that of all others for its dire beauty.'[13]

These lines, with their language of facelessness, of masks, and of regrowth contain a curious echo of plastic surgery, the science which gave new faces to airmen such as Richard Hillary, horribly burned in air accidents. In comparison, 'the long-nosed Blenheim, however, has, literally, no end of a face. Of all planes it possesses most facial features. For instance, it shows clearly a mouth, two wide nostrils, a beaked nose and at least one glaring eyeball.' Yet, in the endlessness of face is the same plasticity of form, seen in Nash's pre-war art, but also in the burns units of the RAF. And just as before, Nash offers another *volte-face* at the end of the essay, as he recalls asking a pilot if he had ever noticed what sort of animal his aeroplane resembled:

He said no, that was a new one on him. 'Well, it's like a shark', I said. 'Good God!' he cried, 'so it is', and took one leap into the cockpit as if he expected it would bite him. As a matter of fact, this shark-face is a superficial resemblance. It depends greatly upon the livid colour of the underparts and the fishlike eyeball.

The animal resemblances, Nash seems to be suggesting, are misleading. While on the ground, and at close quarters, all these aircraft had personalities; but once these machines spluttered to life at the flick of a switch, and climbed into the cold, thin air toward missions that sometimes culminated in success and more often ended in death, their personalities merged with the air-crew who flew them, and bestowed names upon them, in a practice that went back to the Great War. At the beginning of his commission, Nash wrote to a friend: 'Over my head in the wide sky sail my strange creatures impersonally with their impersonal crews of

Paul Nash, *Raiders on the Shore* (1940).

light-hearted boys all bent on varieties of murder.'[14] The most curious aspect of this is that at the very point he imagines the men above, held tight in the fuselage, his vision moves to the impersonal, as if the flesh of the crew is inseparable from the machine; effectively they are the creature's brain and nerves, directing its movements and actions sublimely from within. Hence, despite Nash's best efforts to personalize and anthropomorphize aircraft, his work for the Ministry of Air simply reflects a mortal inevitability.

In his later, more famous oil paintings, such as *Totes Meer* and *Battle of Britain August–October, 1940*, the machines of the Luftwaffe and the RAF are on the edge of disappearance; in the former, the markings of downed German aircraft sink into a sea of heaped wreckage; in the latter, only the cruciform shapes of their wings, set in a sequence of vapour trails and smoke screens, identify the banks of raiders above, and the defenders below. Both canvases suggest that the unique personality of an aircraft – or any object, for that matter – is only ever subsumed into more powerful elements, or larger structures, be they ideological, architectural, or artistic. Indeed, as an object of aesthetics, it may be that fixed-wing aircraft are simply too fragile to bear close scrutiny. In *Raiders*, Nash's first batch of paintings for the Ministry, flying machines are shown to be the most delicate of things, easily lost, blown away, splintered and fractured, scattered on the winds, buried in the fields, eroded by the currents. And as they disappear into the clouds, they take with them the personalities of those souls strapped into them, leaving unfulfilled desires to echo around the now deserted hangars.

Vladimir Tatlin's flying machine, *Letatlin*, constructed in 1929–32.

Panamarenko, *Das Flugzeug* (1967): aluminium tubes, steel wire, rubber driving belt, two adapted bicycle wheels, leather saddle, pedals, Styropor wings covered with canvas.

Artificial Flight

Shortly after its completion in 1932, the Russian Constructivist Vladimir Tatlin had to find a way of explaining his contraption *Letatlin* to officials of the Party that had funded it; rather than setting out its design features, he said simply: 'I have made it as an artist.'[15] *Letatlin* – its name a collision between *Letat*, the Russian word for flight, and Tatlin's name – was a flying machine deriving from experimental designs by Leonardo da Vinci and, more recently, by Otto Lilienthal. 'I want to give back to man the feeling of flight', continued Tatlin. 'We have been robbed of this by the mechanical flight of the aeroplane. We cannot feel the movement of our body in the air.' Hence, his aircraft would be 'an everyday object for the Soviet masses, an ordinary item of use'. He claimed *Letatlin* for his artistic vocation, because by 1932 aviation no longer drew upon individual human effort. His approach to the project was not the engineer's moulding of materials into a prede-termined design, but rather the exploration of the innate qualities of wood, cork, duralumin, silken cord, steel cable, whalebone and leather, and the articulation of them into a shape with minimal reference to contemporary developments in aerodynamics; to create, in other words, a flying machine unencumbered by laws of mechanical and aero-engineering.

Obviously, *Letatlin* never flew, but its spirit has emerged more recently in the work of Panamarenko, who also seeks to rescue flight from the engineers and return it to artisans, creating machines for looking at the world from new angles. One of his earliest and most important works, *Flugzeug*, first exhibited in Düsseldorf in 1968, evokes the technology of the Wright Flyer in the style of Jacques Tati. A modified bicycle frame is connected by means of long rubber drive-belts to two sets of three-bladed rotary wings at either end of the contraption; at the centre of the craft a tiny saddle and drop handlebars, cannibalized from a racing bike, provide accommodation for the busy pilot. Sitting on the gallery floor, this machine seems stranded between light engineering and curatorial aesthetics; between the certainty that this will never fly, and the artist's fervent desire that it is actually capable of leaving the ground; between the fact that it is grounded, as long as the exhibition runs, and the likelihood that it might be blown over by the slightest breeze from an air-conditioning unit.[16]

Perhaps it needs artists to remodel aircraft to the human scale, drawing out such flaws as they have, and so rescue them from the clutches of authority and technology. Indeed, since scale aircraft modelling exists in a cocoon of idealized perfection, amounting to the construction of the perfect specimen or, at the very least, a machine that need not observe the rules of gravity, its pursuit is an expression of a longing for comprehensibility and stability. The 1991 installation, *Himmel*, by the German artist Peter Sauerer is based on just such a conception of stillness – an eternity of stasis – which he obtains not only by translating drama into miniature, but also by means of a sense of process; or, rather, of parallel method. First he fabricates a pair of minutely detailed wooden models of the McDonnell Douglas F-15 Eagle, an air-superiority fighter designed to take control of the upper reaches of the sky and then hold them against any intruder. The machine's technological edge was simple: it was designed around a wing of large area and aerodynamic elegance, into which was inserted a powerplant whose thrust exceeded the aircraft's weight, with the effect that the Eagle could accelerate vertically; the fastest way to Heaven. Although accurate representations of the formal outline of the F-15, the upper surfaces of these models are minutely adorned with architectural perspectives, vertiginous

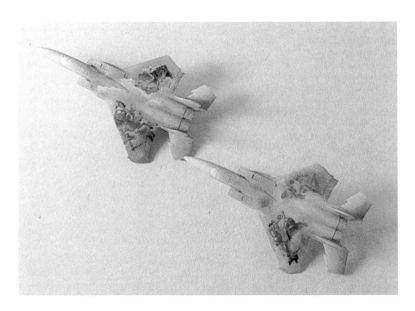

Peter Sauerer, *Himmel* (1991).

A pair of McDonnell Douglas F-15 fighters flying low over the coast. This aircraft, which first came into service in the mid-1970s, quickly established itself as the finest jet fighter ever built.

foreshortenings, and figures of angels and putti clinging to billowing clouds in the midst of an azure sky. The closer one looks at the models hanging side by side in the gallery the clearer Sauerer's intention becomes, since the Eagles double as a pair of plaster fragments fallen from a Tiepolo frieze. This compelling installation perhaps implies how the fate of these earlier objects determines the creation of later technological artefacts. On each model, one of the wings is clipped, to show a jagged edge to the air and to compromise its aerodynamic efficiency, so that the installation itself seems only provisionally held together, and the Eagles appear to be on the edge of falling apart altogether, subject to the destruction attendant upon powered flight.

In *The Sound Barrier*, Ridgefield's son, Chris (Denholm Elliott), dies in a Gypsy Moth on his first solo flight. On the same day that his coffin is interred in the family plot, another box arrives at the aircraft maker's house. Ridgefield, knowing what it contains, eagerly removes the lid and burrows into the tissue paper insulating the object within. Slowly his hand brings out a model aircraft and holds it up to the light streaming in from the window. It is the Ridgefield 902 (in reality, a Supermarine Attacker, the

John Ridgefield flies a model of the 902 – in fact, a Supermarine Attacker – across the face of Daedalus in *The Sound Barrier* (1952).

precursor of the Swift), its fuselage gently tapered, perfectly silvered, and its laminar wings standing sharp. As Ridgefield holds the object at arm's length, yawing it this way and that, Lean frames the shot so that the tiny aircraft appears to be flying into one of the many treasures that adorn the study: a bust of Daedalus, the mythical constructor of flying machinery.

In 'Model Airplanes', a typically mischievous essay by Nicholson Baker, a writer who takes the Nabokovian injunction to 'caress the detail' to its farthest extreme, it is plausibly suggested that 'despite the compensating attractions of glue, the activity of model construction goes to its final rest in one's memory as a long, gradual disappointment.' When one removes the lid, having gazed, just long enough, at the 'Airfix art' on the box top, it is akin to entering an exhibition space: 'Straight from the store, these kits are museums: Kremlins and Smithsonians of the exploded view . . . Nothing is hidden on these architectures; all the complex curves of wings and tailpieces are there, but everything is "straightened up".'[17] As one moves along the plastic sprues, scrutinizing the vaguely familiar relics of a Supermarine Spitfire, or a Lockheed Starfighter, it is a short step from museum to cathedral: 'A pilot, adroitly sliced in two, headless, awaits recomposition in one crowded narthex. The elegant landing gear, twice as impressive as the real thing, is on view in the south transept.' The box effectively becomes ' the basilica of the unbuilt', in which 'you are content to wander these galleries of imaginary hobbyistic space'. Yet, Baker suggests, the longer one ponders the parts of the aircraft, imagining them coming together to form a perfect miniature whole, the less likely it will be that the model will ever be assembled. While constructed model aircraft mimic the fragility of the real thing, so that their wings are easily clipped, or broken, it seems that unconstructed models are stronger, *ceteris paribus*, than the objects of which they are scaled

down representations; designed and fabricated, but still in pieces, they are ideal forms, to be propelled into the air by imagination, that most potent and volatile fuel – after modelling glue, at least. Fundamentally, then the activity of model making, of creating a machine that cannot fly in the air but only in the mind, offers the opportunity, if not the time, to imagine the imperfect perfect.

However, Baker suggests, when one is faced with a box of tricky stealth technology – the component parts of the Northrop B-2 Spirit, for instance – the issue becomes more problematic. Althoughthe full-scale 'Stealth Bomber' is beautiful from a distance, 'in a worrisomely Transylvanian sort of way', it is 'the result of astounding advances in computer-aided design and manufacturing processes'. Since even the slightest distortion in its surface panels would compromise the bomber's stealth characteristics, and the smallest changes to its exterior shape might cause turbulence that could ruin a long-range mission, the outer skin panels of the

A Northrop B-2 Spirit, named 'The Spirit of Georgia', being prepared for flight.

Spirit are largely bonded together, and then 'glued' to the airframe before final assembly, to ensure a seamless finish and blemish-free surface. Gazing at the parts, Baker is struck by the fact that the Spirit's 'continuous curves and unmitigated blackness' make for a disappointing scale model. Its surface is so 'maddeningly smooth, that its featurelessness soaks up the eager radar of the visual sense' and so denies the modeller any sense of 'drag'; that is, all those 'rivets, knobs, holes, wires, hinges, visible missiles, sensors, gun blisters – all those encrustations that inspire study, and make imitation' worth pursuing. Because the Spirit, 'the result of composite-molding machinery, itself too closely approximates the fluent, impressionable greatness of molded styrene', it is, effectively, *already* a model. Since a scale model of it would be unable to demonstrate 'the extraordinary talent plastic has for the mimicry of other materials and textures', the consequence is that the Stealth Bomber, the perfect example of artificial flight, is inimitable and unreproducible; simply beyond capture.

Sir Hiram Maxim's 'Captive Flying Machine', at the Pleasure Beach, Blackpool, Lancashire, pictured here on a 1908 postcard, was opened in August 1904, and remains in service to this day.

In 1932 Norman Bel Geddes observed: 'Keats wrote a few immortal lines about a Grecian urn. Had he known about it, and felt like it, he could have written them about an airplane.'[18] A fascinating conjunction, this; but if the designer had read to the end of the poem, it would have been clear that the fundamental concepts it applies to Greek vases – silent form, endless perdurability, timeless perfection – were not applicable to airframes, especially those machines that, buried deep in earth and water, only emerge through the efforts of aviation archaeologists. Yet 'What mad pursuit? What struggle to escape?' two of the rhetorical questions posed by Keats of that ancient vessel, might easily be directed to some of the more visionary flying machine designs of the last century.

At Blackpool's Pleasure Beach, hidden amid the high-tech theme rides, there remains one of the most extraordinary aeronautical designs Britain has ever seen. Sir Hiram Maxim's 'Captive Flying Machine' came into service in August 1904, six months after the Wright Brothers' first flight, and is still in use today. A steel pole 19 m (62 ft) high supports ten arms, from which hang carriages that spread outwards as the ride revolves under the power of two 50 hp electric motors, so creating the illusion of flying. It is a suitable monument to the man whose ideas of flight were grand enough for him to claim that he first flew eight years before the American pair.

Maxim was of French Huguenot descent but of American birth, and first came to Europe in 1881 as the representative of the US Electric Light Company; while in Paris on their behalf he invented the Maxim gun, which he imported to England, where it was developed further. In 1887 Maxim, now a wealthy man, began to design an aeroplane, which he estimated would cost £100,000 and take some five years to build. He rented a large open space at Baldwyns Park, Bexley, Kent, where he erected the first aircraft

hangar in England and a wind tunnel. In the years that followed he worked on various designs, including his own steam engine, for which he developed a laminated wood propeller, a form of construction that was to become standard practice. His aim was to build a massive machine to carry a load of several thousand pounds, saying, 'It is much easier to manoeuvre a machine of great length than one which is very short.' Maxim's contraption was a quasi-aeroplane, having biplane wings with dihedral on the outer panels and two primitive elevators, with a total area of 4,000 square feet; two 180 horsepower steam engines each driving a propeller nearly 5 metres (18 ft) in diameter; and an all-up weight of more than 31 tons, including a crew of three. Maxim was wise enough to understand that getting a machine airborne and controlling it once flying were two different things, so his machine was guided by rails, 550 m (1,800 ft) long. While allowing a degree of 'free' flight, these restrained any serious deviation from the straight and narrow and prevented the need to rebuild the craft from scratch in the event of a crash, as had faced so many other experimenters. On the Biplane's third test run, on 31 July 1894, with Maxim and a crew of three aboard, the boilers were stoked to deliver a boost in pressure to the engines until, when exceeding

Sir Hiram Maxim's aeroplane, pictured in the verdant surroundings of Baldwyns Park, Bexley, Kent, in 1894.

70 km/h (42 mph), the whole structure lifted into the air with such force that it broke the restraining track and flew along for about 60 metres (200 ft), at roughly the height achieved by the Wright brothers on their first flight eight years later at Kitty Hawk. The plane crashlanded, severely damaged, but its crew escaped without injury. Satisfied with this achievement, Maxim now abandoned his experiments and started to design fairground rides, scoffing at the feeble attempts at flight others were making. In 1908 he stated that, in all the successful aeroplanes that had flown since 1894, 'practically no essential departure has been made from my original lines', and that 'indicates to my mind that I had reasoned out the best type of a machine even before I commenced a stroke of the work'.[19]

Two decades later, Claude Dornier, the designer of the world's largest and heaviest aircraft, the Do-X, had reasoned out every detail of his plane before he would launch it on the world. Before building the prototype Dornier, a cautious and artistic man, and a team of carpenters built a full-size wooden mock-up of it in a hangar, to make sure everything would fit – common practice later in the century, but singular then. He also ran static tests to see if the main spar was strong enough and, like Maxim, built a rig on which to test the engine installations. Empty it displaced 33 tons, and 61 loaded; its six tanks contained 21,000 gallons of fuel, and its wings, as aerodynamically efficient as ironing boards, spanned almost 50 metres (160 ft). It was propelled by twelve Bristol Jupiter air-cooled engines, British designed but built under licence by Siemens in Germany, mounted in six 'push-pull' pairs on a network of struts, high above the wing, and spinning out almost 6,000 hp. When it was discovered that these were underpowered, and overheating, they were replaced with twelve American Curtiss engines, more powerful but considerably heavier owing to the plumbing for the water-cooling. The duralumin hull had three

decks; the ten-man crew was housed on the uppermost, close to the engines, while the lower reaches had been insulated and partitioned to create several sleeping cabins, as well as a well-appointed and deeply carpeted lounge with a gramophone that could be played if conditions were smooth enough. In addition, there was a 'recreation room', a bathroom, a smoking room, a kitchen and a little dining-room. In normal service, Dornier intended his great machine to carry about 72 passengers.

The Do-X set off for its proving flight from Lake Constance in November 1930 under the command of Captain Friedrich Christiansen, with a crew of nineteen and carrying a load of mail. They stopped at Amsterdam, and at Calshot on Southampton Water, but on heading south into the Bay of Biscay they flew into fog and had to put down at sea, and taxi, rather than fly, into Bordeaux harbour. At Lisbon a fuel tank in the wing caught fire; repairs lasted a month. Once the machine was up and running again, Christiansen tried to take off from Las Palmas in the Canaries in a high swell, and

The Dornier Do-X flying-boat, on a proving flight on Lake Constance, 1930.

battered the hull so badly that repairs this time took three months. By now, the crew were beginning to realize that the Dornier, however docile in the cool climates of northern Europe, was behaving differently in the thick tropical air. The next leg, from the Cape Verde Islands to South America, was 2,250 km (1,400 miles), and to ensure they made their destination they now had to leave behind half the crew and everything else expendable, including the cargo of mailbags. Even so, for the first part of the flight the Do-X, held down by the suction created by air trapped between the wings and the waves, flew along at just 6 metres (20 ft) above sea level. The aircraft travelled as far as Rio, before turning northwards along the Pan Am flying-boat route up through the West Indies to Miami. Ten months after it left Germany, the Do-X arrived in New York harbour on 27 August 1931, to a ticker-tape welcome; it had covered 20,000 km (12,000 miles) at an average speed of 3 km (1.6 mph). The following May, the Do-X was towed out into Manhasset Bay for the start of her long, long take-off run for the return trip to Germany, via Newfoundland and the Azores. Once back in her native land, after almost 18 months' absence, the aircraft was given another grand welcome, before quietly being sent to the Berlin air museum, where it remained largely intact until an Allied bomb destroyed it in 1942.[20]

The Dornier's distinctive if profoundly unairworthy shape, praised by, among others, Norman Bel Geddes, would later emerge in Eduardo Paolozzi's small, beautifully modelled sculpture, *A Short History of Alternate Worlds* (1990). A minutely detailed model of the aircraft, three feet in length and fabricated out of tin sheeting, is attended by twenty-four clay figures, tinted blue and brown, standing in ranks, in no discernible sequence, either side of its streamlined prow. Its great flattened wings are surmounted by another six, male and female, matching the number of engine nacelles. Perhaps the sculpture toys with oppositions, both abstract

– plan and accident; movement and stasis; strength and fragility – and physical – air and water; push and pull. Yet it's also possible to see it as a nostalgic valediction to the lost aeronautical vision that such machines, however chaotic in their flight characteristics, were intended to create; a vision of a new order, which might connect disparate worlds and provide models of progress. At the time the Dornier first flew, such designs were usually authored by a single person. Within a couple of years, however, any artistry in conception was being eroded by the creation of machines conceived and executed by a collective will to power.

In Britain, during the latter stages of the war, an Inter-Departmental Committee was established, under the chairmanship of the aviation pioneer Lord Brabazon of Tara, to consider the types of civil aircraft required in the immediate post-war period. The

Eduardo Paolozzi, *A Short History of Alternate Worlds*, 1990.

Committee recommended that the first of the five projects, a luxury transatlantic airliner, massive in scale, was to have priority. Given its size, a firm already building large bombers would receive the contract. In 1941, in response to an Air Ministry brief, Bristol, the long-lived aircraft company responsible for the Blenheim, had designed an intercontinental bomber, clean as a sailplane, with a V-tail, a slender fuselage and a great thick wing with eight of Bristol's own radial engines, entirely buried within and geared in pairs to drive pusher propellers mounted on stalks behind the wing. Too radical, too heavy, it was rejected. However, one member of the Committee, a senior Air Ministry civil servant charged with gathering performance data, remembered this singular design and tabled it as the model for a transatlantic airliner. The Committee saw the possibilities, and commissioned Bristol to build the prototype, informing them that 'financial conditions must, necessarily, be secondary'.[21]

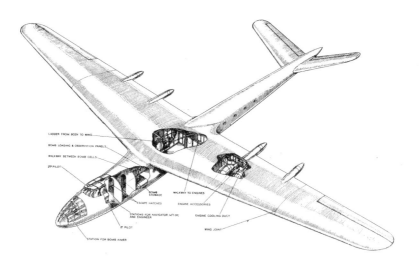

The Bristol Aircraft Company's proposed design for a heavy bomber, 1942, technically ambitious and swiftly rejected.

The re-design submitted in 1944 promised a supremely beautiful flying machine, with a long slender fuselage of constantly varying cross-section, and a most elegant curved and pointed fin. The wing was huge, and so immensely thick that engineers gaining access from the fuselage would be able to walk upright inside it to inspect the eight 2500 hp Bristol Centaurus radial engines, which were coupled through gearboxes in pairs to drive four sets of double contra-rotating airscrews. These engines developed a total of 20,000 hp at full power. At this time, the Brabazon was the biggest aircraft in the world; it was fully 15 metres (50 ft) high to the top of its fin, and, weighing 70 tons empty, was designed to operate at an all-up-weight of almost double that figure.

A vast new hangar, large enough to accommodate the construction of three Brabazons, was erected at the Filton factory, while the company extended its runway, even though this would involve closing a newly completed dual carriageway bypass and the demolition of part of Charlton village, including its pub and

The Bristol Brabazon on a test flight over Gloucestershire, 1949.

post office. A full-scale wooden model of the aeroplane was constructed, joiners making use of expensive and rare mahogany from Honduras; the mock-up was more like that expected of an ocean liner than an airliner, where weight counted for everything. The thinking behind it was similar to that behind the flying-boat; passengers were to have the kind of freedom they had on a ship. According to Bristol publicity, the mock-up contained 'a most magnificent ladies' powder room with wooden aluminium-painted mirrors and even receptacles for the various lotions and powders used by the modern young lady'.

The Brabazon's first flight took place on 4 September 1949, witnessed by 10,000 spectators and a press contingent 300 strong. As its needle-tipped nose slowly lifted from the runway the BBC's aviation correspondent exclaimed, 'She's off!'; and as the great aircraft banked away from the factory, a group of senior RAF officers were seen to break ranks and celebrate by throwing their caps into the air. Overwhelmed, and perhaps forgetting the connotations, the BBC commentator described the Brabazon overhead as 'a giant silver albatross'. Over the next few weeks, the aircraft was flown on short hops in southern England. It was demonstrated at the Farnborough Air Show and the attendees were much impressed by its impeccable finish; on Bank Holidays, it was flown low around the seaside resorts on the south coast so that the Great British Public could see the model of luxury engineering their tax contributions had funded; and when a group of Bristol's engineers visited a London theatre on a works outing, the audience, tipped off by the management, treated them to a standing ovation.

Yet although the Brabazon had completed only several hundred hours' flying, hairline cracks had already been discovered in the engine mounts. Just like the Comet, another design recommended by the Brabazon Committee and then being developed by de

Havilland, the Brabazon had been conceived before the problem of metal fatigue had been fully understood. Metallurgical analysis predicted that, at this rate, the airframe would have a 'fatigue life' of only 5,000 hours, an absurd figure for an airliner whose economics depended on the concept that it made money only when in flight. Then, in February 1952, the Minister of Supply, Duncan Sandys, announced that 'in view of the poor economic state of the country', work on the Brabazon was 'temporarily' suspended, to continue 'when conditions became more favourable'. They never were; fifteen months later he announced that 'neither civil airlines nor fighting services could foresee any economic use' for an aircraft of this size, so the prototype and a half-finished Mark II as well as their construction jigs were sold off for scrap metal. All that remains now of the project is a piece of fuselage bearing the Brabazon's name, which ended up at the Bristol Industrial Museum, and a spare nosewheel assembly, which was placed in a glass case in the Science Museum and connected to a hydraulic pump, to retract and extend at the press of a button: a very model of the pointlessness the Brabazon's grand design came to represent.

Appropriate Tech

In 1975, as his architectural practice took off with the construction of the Willis Faber and Dumas building in Ipswich, Norman Foster gained a Pilot's Licence, the ambition of a lifetime. He later explained that, as a child growing up in the industrial suburbs of wartime Manchester, close to the Avro factory, he had become 'obsessed by the world of model aircraft', until one day, as he peered through the park railings, the model materialized: 'Standing upright with its nose buried in the ground was the unmistakable shape of a fighter with its RAF roundels painted on

the fuselage.' Over half a century later he was still unable to decide 'if this was a dream that cannot be forgotten, or whether I imagined a painting by Paul Nash, which had come alive'.[22] Among his associates there was little surprise that, when approached by the BBC to nominate his favourite building, Foster chose the Boeing 747, defending his seemingly perverse choice with the argument that, even though the Jumbo jet 'blurs the distinction between technology and building' because it flies, 'with about 3,000 square feet of floorspace, fifteen lavatories, three kitchens and a capacity for up to 367 guests, this is surely a true building'.[23]

To be precise, Foster's preferred building is a high tech, low-wing monoplane, its great wings swept back like its predecessor, the 707, with a 59.4 m (195 ft) span and an area of nearly 6,000 square feet and its four engines slung low in streamlined nacelles,

Boeing models: an array of design proposals for the 747.

generating in excess of 90 tonnes (200,000 lb) of thrust. Its long fuselage (70 m or 231 ft, nose to tail) has a circular cross-section (6 m or 19 ft 5 in wide), with a height of 2.5 metres (8 ft 4 in) for the main cabin, and an upper deck, housing the crew compartment and a forward lounge section, reached by a spiral staircase, as in the old Boeing Stratocruiser derived from the B-29 bomber. In profile, the designers created a parabolic nose, the upper arc of which gradually slanted downward to the main cabin tubular section, and tapered away to end in a conical tail section, higher than a six-storey building. The combination made the 747 the most aerodynamically efficient transport ever designed. Indeed, enthusiasts have even likened its shape to fighter aircraft: Clive James thinks it has the look of the F-86 Sabre, with 'its flight-deck bulge perched right forward like a Sabre's bubble canopy and the same proud angle to its tail feathers'.[24] Yet Foster is unable to countenance the possibility that mere aerodynamics gave this piece of industrial architecture its heroic outer form.

> This thing was designed. In fact an engineer called Joseph Sutter is credited as the chief designer. It is not decorated; it has style, by which I mean metaphoric elements associated with cultural ideas of speed, efficiency, power, strength, dependability – and yet it is genuinely beautiful. I believe all modern architecture is capable of this intrinsic style and beauty without compromising its function.[25]

In 1997, in an essay written to accompany a first-day cover of five Royal Mail postage stamps dedicated to 'Architects of the Air', Foster went still further, and claimed: 'Aviation started as an offspring of the engineering that makes a work of architecture possible, borrowing freely at the time from the established disciplines. In a remarkably short period it has grown up to be bigger and faster, generating technology and a body of knowledge which are now invaluable to the parent.'[26] Many of Foster's finest buildings are material restatements of this reciprocity, and as such his structurally rational work has frequently been described as 'High Tech'. The mischievous critic, Reyner Banham, however, had reservations about the term, and in an essay on Foster in 1979 termed it 'appropriate tech'.[27]

He well understood the appropriateness of technology, since in 1939 Banham, a seventeen-year-old school leaver, enrolled on a scholarship at Bristol Technical College, where he trained as an aero engineer before taking up a post at the Bristol Aeroplane Company's Engine Division as a fitter. He worked throughout the war, mainly on the Mercury powerplants for Blenheims but also on the Perseus engines for the Brabazon until, in 1945 he suffered a nervous breakdown: 'Well you can't go on doing 24 hour shifts one after another forever and just before the end of the war I was invalided out.'[28] On leaving Bristol, Banham decided to recast himself as an architectural commentator, but he would never forget the design aesthetic of the machines on which he spent so much of his apprenticeship. In 1962 he flew back from Australia, via the west coast of the US, and had an opportunity to sample several airliners. The Douglas DC-6B, with 'prehistoric-type dahlia-shaped piston engines', was mechanically and structurally as sound as a bell; comfortable, not cramped; surprisingly quiet. Designed with 'innate style by people who cared about designing airliners and built a good one', it flew with 'authority'.[29] At the other extreme, the Vickers Viscount seemed to have been designed with no thoughts beyond load-factors and paying seats. Cramped and badly finished, it was the profit-motive with wings. After this, he looked forward to the Big Dougs, the new DC-8 jets of United Airlines that would transport him eastward:

The DC-8s did not disappoint – they are the aircraft that set the standard by which all other jets fail. Again, built like tanks with professionalism in every detail (you should see those patterns of rivet heads on the wing!); an interior plainer and better-detailed than that of a London bus; all ancillary services built into the backs of the simple leather-covered seats, no overhead clutter; no patterned surfaces and only a little veneer; and a gait as steady as a tea-trolley on a pile carpet.[30]

The interior design here had been modelled by Raymond Loewy, who had been engaged by United to restyle its corporate identity, and assist in the selection and equipping of their forthcoming jet fleet to be termed Mainliners. He created flexible track seating, serving trays and tables for the cabin, and a new livery, the red and pale blue lines of which followed the shape of the windows and the tail.[31] For Banham, clearly, the overall effect was coolly modern, effortlessly direct, in direct contrast to the Boeing 707, which though comparable in size, was 'a mass of neurotic twitches', doubtless derived from its origins in the company's jet bomber programme.[32]

'The aircraft that set the standard': A Douglas DC-8, in the colours of United Airlines, early 1960s.

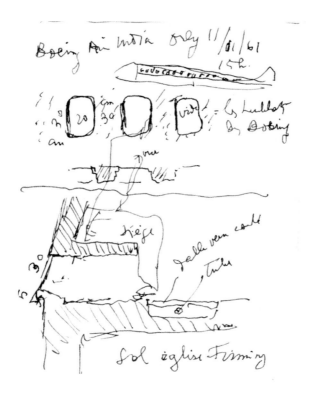

Le Corbusier, too had little affection for the Boeing; nevertheless, anticipating Foster's paean to the interior fittings of the later 747 model, he once sketched the portholes and the ventilation nozzles of a 707 with a view to incorporating them into the fabric of the unfinished church at Firminy.[33] Of course, deriving architectural inspiration from aerospace engineering had been attempted more or less whimsically since the earliest days of flight, but it is Le Corbusier who most obsessively charts the connections between aircraft design and architecture. In a famous essay published in *L'Ésprit nouveau*, the journal he edited with Amédée Ozenfant, he considers the architectural products made by Maison Voisin, the

A page from one of Le Corbusier's sketchbooks, showing his impressions of the cabin windows of a Boeing 707 above notes for the commission at Firminy.

company established by Gabriel Voisin, which had constructed more than 10,000 reconnaissance aircraft between 1915 and 1918. After the Armistice, in an attempt to stave off imminent bankruptcy, the firm sought to diversify and exhibited several prototypes of prefabricated housing. Le Corbusier's interest in this technology was characteristically precise though its architectural distinction was negligible; simply, Voisin was now producing houses that did not need to be built on an excavated foundation, but could simply be erected, and then 'chocked' into place. Hence, the dwelling was no longer fixed. This simple technology, emerging out of Fordist lines of production, now opened new routes for his own projects and practices, at every level. Le Corbusier and Ozenfant announced, triumphantly:

> Impossible to wait on the slow collaboration of the successive efforts of excavator, mason, carpenter, joiner, tiler, plumber . . . houses must go up all of a piece, made by machine tools in a factory, assembled as Ford assembles cars, on moving conveyor belts. Aviation is achieving prodigies of serial production . . . It is in aircraft factories that the soldier-architects have decided to build the houses; they decided to build this house like an aircraft, with the same structural methods, lightweight framing, metal braces, tubular supports.[34]

At this stage, shortly after the Great War, Le Corbusier was not drawn to the aircraft as a means to the simplest of ends, the ascent into the sky. Instead, his interest was largely academic, concerned with 'the insertion of architecture into the contemporary conditions of production'. Hence the lightness, economy and speed that the aircraft industry could bring to bear on building was, in effect, synonymous with what came to be known as *l'ésprit nouveau*. Although the housing Voisin was advertising was little more than a large steel-framed shed, with a pitched roof, Le Corbusier saw in its fabrication the basis of a design ethos that could form an ideal for living; in effect, it was material proof that 'the aeroplane is a little house that can fly and resist the storm'.[35]

It was from the opportunist thinking of *L'Ésprit Nouveau* that Le Corbusier created perhaps his best-known architectural manifesto, *Vers une architecture* (1925), a whole section of which, 'Les Yeux qui ne voient pas II', is devoted to aircraft. No mention is made now of the Voisin proposals praised so highly two years earlier – as it happens, the firm had decided against putting the prefabs into production and had moved into the manufacture of luxury cars. However, the ethos of mobility the product had implied is modified into a basic statement: 'the house is a machine for living in'.[36] Once this tenet is accepted, an aircraft offers an example of a perfect solution to frequently stated architectural problems, and becomes, in effect, a pure form of technical logic: 'The lesson of the airplane is not primarily in the forms it has created, and above all we must learn to see in an airplane not a bird or a dragon-fly, but a machine for flying'.[37] Already it seems that Le Corbusier is warning against the kind of anthropomorphism Nash's whimsical account of raf bombers would exhibit almost two decades later. Indeed, since the invention of the powered flying machine had 'mobilised invention, intelligence and daring: imagination and cold reason', any account of aircraft demanded that myth and prejudice be cast aside. Hence,

the airplane shows us that a problem well stated finds its solution. To wish to fly like a bird is to state the problem baldly, and Ader's Bat never left the ground. To invent a flying machine having in mind nothing alien to pure mechanics, that is to say, to search for a means of suspension in the air and a means of propulsion, was to put the problem properly: in less than ten years the whole world could fly.[38]

Le Corbusier's allusion to the 'Bat' is revealing, in that he is reacting against one of France's strongest myths of flight. On October 1890, in the grounds of the Château d'Armainvilliers, near Paris, the French engineer Clément Ader, sitting behind a compact steam engine in the 'cabin' of his monoplane, the Bat, began to roll along a specially prepared track. The primitive tractor propeller of his machine, made of bamboo, and designed to resemble four giant feathers joined at the middle, would have provided little thrust; the wings, so deeply arched and cambered, and its spars and linkages modelled on the skeleton of the foxbat, generated negligible lift. Yet two minutes into the run, as he boosted the boiler pressure to increase the propeller's speed, Ader suddenly experienced a jolt. The only two witnesses, his assistants in the experiment, later claimed that for the distance of 50 metres (165 ft) the machine was about 20 cm (8 in.) clear of the ground.[39]

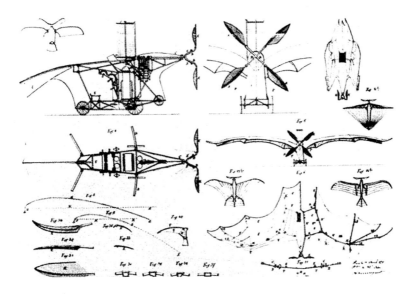

Clément Ader's 'Eole' patent drawings, lodged officially in Paris, 1891

Le Corbusier's scant allusion dismisses Ader's achievements too cheaply – after all, 'Avion', the word which, within a decade or so, would generally denote powered flying machines of the type being venerated in *Vers une architecture*, would be first coined by Ader in 1892 and applied to the frame of the flying machine he built after the Bat had run its course. Furthermore, it is even possible that Ader's was the world's first powered flight. In his commentary on Le Corbusier's passage, Reyner Banham observed: 'Ironically enough the Ader Bat was proved to be just capable of flight before *L'Ésprit nouveau* had ceased publication, and the fact was noted in its pages, without any comment beyond that it contributed to the glory of France as the pioneer country of Aviation.'[40] Even had it flown, it is likely that Ader's aircraft would quickly have crashed: its design allowed only for lift and thrust, and its pilot, his forward vision blocked by the boiler, had no means of controlling it in the air.

Coincidentally, lift and thrust, suspension and propulsion, were the only forces that were interesting Le Corbusier at this date. As Banham points out, 'he does not discuss the problem of penetration in this context, nor that of controls – that is, he states the problem of aviation as Chanute or Lilienthal stated it, but whether he did so with knowledge of their work is not clear'; and his awareness of the physics of flight was as rudimentary as his sense of its history.[41] And once it became clear, as the 1920s rolled on, that the function of power in architecture would rarely matter, other than in terms of elevator shafts and air-conditioning ducts, the concept of suspension, the bearing of load, became the only flight force that mattered to his theories.

Consider the selection of illustrations in 'Les Yeux qui ne voient pas II'. The chapter contains sixteen black-and-white photographs. With one exception, these show aircraft of the previous fifteen years, almost all of the images having been cut and pasted, as per

The Caproni Ca-60, the 'Triple Hydroplane', which crashed on its maiden flight on Lake Maggiore in January 1921.

A Farman Goliath at Croydon airport in 1921. Note the open 'French windows' at the front of the aircraft.

Le Corbusier's usual practice, from the sales literature and brochures circulated by aircraft manufacturers: Spad, Farman, Caproni.[42] Curiously, only one of the illustrations depicts a monoplane, the form in which by 1925 the future of aircraft construction obviously lay. All of the remaining types in the sequence show biplanes and triplanes, including the ill-fated Caproni 60, which he labels the 'Triple Hydroplane'. The size of a tenement block, this aircraft had nine wings, attached to a kind of gigantic houseboat of a hull, and eight 400 hp American Liberty engines, four at the front pulling, and four at the back pushing. When it was launched on Lake Maggiore in January 1921, the pilot managed to take the aircraft up to 20 metres (60 ft) before, lacking a tailplane to provide the necessary flight control, the Caproni stalled and, its ballast shifting, its main wings snapping loose, it ditched onto the 'cold reason' of the lake. It's tempting to suggest that its inclusion here suggested that even pureness of function mattered less than a stunning array of struts and planes.

Siginificantly, half of the photographs Le Corbusier selected were of a single aircraft type: the Farman Goliath. This 'double-decker' was originally conceived as a heavy bomber – or 'bombing machine', as Le Corbusier grimly puts it in a caption – and saw action over German positions in the closing stages of the Great War. Once the hostilities were over, Farman, desperate to continue sales, re-marketed it as an airliner, or 'Air Express' as it is quaintly labelled in the chapter. A Goliath inaugurated the first scheduled London to Paris air service in 1919, completing the journey in two hours. Even by this date, however, the Goliath was an obsolete machine. It was slow, reaching only 200 km/h (130 mph), flat out; noisy, constructed as it was out of wood and canvas; and although well appointed within, its large windows affording a clear view of the skies ahead, the aircraft was desperately uncomfortable

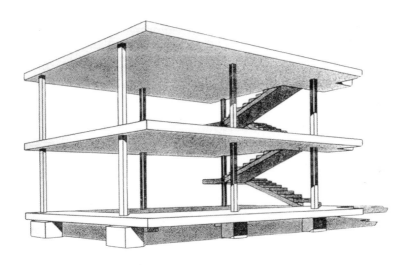

in flight, especially when compared with lighter and more compact monoplanes, such as the Junkers F.13, a machine designed specifically for passenger transport, and which boasted an enclosed, insulated cabin and, as a bonus, seatbelts.

In fact, Le Corbusier's fondness for the clumsy and obsolete Goliath stemmed simply from the fact that its airframe modelled his own architectural and technological advance. *Vers une architecture* claims that if aircraft logic was applied to house building, all the intimidation and mystification of the academy could be simply ignored; like an aircraft, a house would be 'pure function', offering protection from the elements ('heat, cold, rain, thieves and the inquisitive') and acting as 'a receptacle for light and sun.'[43] The illustrations of the Goliath all draw attention to the framework of the aircraft and, cumulatively, there emerges a visual link with one of Le Corbusier's most famous skeletal designs, first published in 1915, the year the Goliath took to the air. Drawings of the

The *Dom-Ino* system, a neologistic combination of domicile and innovation, which is naturally also meant to recall a game of spatial calculation.

'Dom-Ino' system show three horizontal slabs, their edges both supporting and supported by six columns of reinforced concrete (*pilotis*), served by two flights of steps at one end. Since the weight of the floors was borne by the exterior columns, rather than interior pillars, this arrangement created a large space, unencumbered by supports; walls could be pushed out to maximize floor space, and so create the first true open-plan living space. The famous prototype is reproduced in miniature several times in *Vers une architecture*, and is undoubtedly meant to echo, in terms of design at least, the Goliath and other biplanes contemporary with it, replete with their vertical struts edgily supporting horizontally stacked wings.

It is unsurprising, then, that one of the designs on which Le Corbusier was working in 1925 should feature the Goliath so prominently. He had been commissioned by William Cook, an expatriate American journalist who painted in his spare time, to create a house on a small plot of land in Boulogne-sur-Seine. It

Le Corbusier and Pierre Jeanneret designed the Maison Cook in Boulogne-sur-Seine, in 1925. Note the rounded porter's lodge, its shape recalling the nose section of the Goliath.

was a difficult brief, since any facade needed to continue the extant building line, and Cook had specified a number of essential elements: servants' quarters; studio space; integral garage; gardens at ground level, and elsewhere if possible. Le Corbusier's response was simple, and immediately recognizable from *Vers une architecture*. He placed the living accommodation in an elegant cube, one of those ideal forms also singled out in the book, and raised it up above ground level on side walls and on a centre line of three cylindrical *pilotis*, the foremost one visible in the front view. The upper façade of white stucco was penetrated by a horizontal arrow of dark, opaque glazing; a row of windows in flight from the world. Kenneth Frampton has described how the 'representational façade is reduced to a taut asymmetrical machine-like membrane . . . analogous to the stretched fabric of an aircraft'.[44] This building, however, an exquisite combination of imagination and cold reason, demands more precision than the simplicity of analogy. For in the centre of the façade at ground level, acting accommodatingly as a porter's lodge, is the forward fuselage section of the Farman Goliath 'Air Express'. As in the 'Dom-Ino' scheme, the ground below and the first floor above echo the lower and upper wing, respectively, of the great French biplane, while the *pilotis* undertake the key role of supporting struts, bracing the machine as it propels itself into the future of modern space.

Air Shows

'The airplane, symbol of the New Age . . . The airplane, advance guard of the conquering armies of the New Age, the airplane', Le Corbusier proclaimed in *Aircraft*, a publication that is, in effect, the prospectus of a non-existent air show.[45] Certainly, the aviation exhibitions of the inter-war period became an important point of departure for his aesthetic; it was from the first such event in Paris after the Great War that Le Corbusier dates his own ecstatic feeling of 'the new era of machine civilization'. At the central point of the book there is an image taken at the Milan Aeronautical Exhibition of 1934, at the opening of which Mussolini proclaimed that 'a country's aviation can be great, average or small, according as the public consciousness of aviation is great, average or small'. Le Corbusier glosses these words by explaining that this was 'an appeal to participate, and the Milan Exhibition a spell, alert, conquering and joyous'.[46] The exhibition, which contained rooms devoted to Air Power in the Libyan War, to D'Annunzio, to Aviation and Fascism and to Icarus, also included the famous Sala delle Medaglie d'Oro, designed by Marcello Nizzoli and Edoardo Persico. The room, bathed in 'unreal light', contained a forest of white wooden lattices, supporting a large number of graphic and photographic reproductions of Italian aircraft in flight, which 'appeared to float in space and to advance and recede throughout the depth of the hall'.[47]

Le Corbusier's response to the exhibition's appeal that he participate in an ongoing aeronautical debate is best seen in his displaying of aircraft at Expos in the late 1930s. Take, for example, the proposal made in early 1937 for the Bata pavilion for the Exposition Internationale des Arts et Techniques dans la Vie Moderne in Paris, which demanded that a full-size Zlín Z-XII monoplane, an aircraft produced by a subsidiary of the Czech shoe firm, be suspended from the pavilion's ceiling.[48] The scheme was rejected, but similar elements of aviation then emerged into his epoch-making 'Pavillon des Temps Nouveaux', another installation created for the same event. The external design and the materials of this pavilion, constructed out of canvas and supported by

Le Corbusier's Bata pavilion conceived for the Paris Expo 1937, but uncommissioned, envisaged the suspension of a Zlín aircraft from the roof.

The interior of Le Corbusier's Pavillon des Temps Nouveaux, erected for the Paris Expo 1937.

latticework pylons, obviously allude to contemporary aircraft construction, but as the visitor entered the pavilion through the aerofoil profile of the pivoted door, the debts to aviation became still stronger: in the centre of the space, mounted on an 3 metre (9 ft) pole, was a scale model of a Bloch 174 twin-engined bomber, an aircraft which would not fly until the following year, but which was considered impressive enough to be kept in production by the Germans after the French surrender in 1940.[49]

Despite the critical success of the pavilion once the Expo opened, Le Corbusier perhaps realized that the aeroplane mounted so centrally in his exhibition space had been rather overshadowed by those orbiting in the space of the 'Pavillon de l'Air', a short walk to the north. This building, located before the Esplanade des Invalides, opposite the Pont Alexandre-III, was designed by Audout, Harwig, Gerodias, and constructed out of metal and glass to create what was, in effect, a glazed hangar in the shape of a bomber's upended nose section. (In its conception this design may owe something to Pierre Chareau's Maison de Verre, constructed in 1931; and it is possible that the array of concentric hoops, creating a dome, may have anticipated Foster's Reichstag.) Certainly, the Pavilion looked rather more striking by night than during the day, as the lights illuminated the bizarre internal structures. Inside, a series of circular gantries, fashioned in the form of tubes, permitted visitors to navigate the central space of the arena and to inspect, at various heights and at close quarters, large scale models of the latest French military aircraft, either suspended from the roof or mounted on poles. The central example, yet another Bloch 174, was encircled by two large coloured rings, placed at right angles to one another, and these in turn were held within the bigger tube. The rings implied suspension within a predictable orbit; the tubular walkway propulsion along a planned route. Taken

The interior of the Pavillon de l'Air, constructed for the Paris Expo, 1937. Note the murals by Robert and Sonia Delaunay adorning the walls.

together, they demarcated a gyroscope, a means of navigation perfected to achieve blind flight; movement without frontiers.

The interior arrangement, so highly praised at the time by Le
Corbusier (among many others), had been designed by Robert
Delaunay and Felix Aublet. As a further contribution to the
Pavilion, Delaunay and his wife Sonia created several murals, each
containing vibrantly abstract circles, box-like forms and dazzling
streaks to create a fresh homage to the inventors and technical
developments that had made aviation possible. Since his attend-
ance at the Paris Aeronautical Exhibition back in 1909, Delaunay
had consistently sought to create a means by which the technological world of the time could understand itself, and this was now
developed to its fullest extent in *Propellers and Rhythm*, a gouache
executed shortly after the completion of the Pavilion. In it,
Delaunay combines the flat air-like prisms of his mural on the rear
wall of the 'conical hall' with the three-dimensional rings arrayed
in the hall's central space. These circles are clearly intended to
materialize the flight paths of aircraft just visible in the area, but
necessarily they recall valves, wheels, propellers and shift levers in
the cockpit; precisely the objects visualized in his wife's murals.
But as ever in Delaunay's work, the painted forms remain symbolic
of, and in conformity with, the principles of the machine aesthetic; they are only meant as an analogy to – not as a model of
– those war machines placed so prominently on display in the
'Pavillon de l'Air'.

There is a curiosity about aircraft displayed in static interior
tableaux, since they are so much out of their element as to be
rendered inert. The drama of Norman Foster's design for the
American Air Museum at Duxford, a facility which now holds one
of the finest collections of military planes outside the US, lies in the
way it suggests that the exhibits of the collection are not fixed,

but might easily take off again. The airfield, close to Cambridge, was established as an RAF station in 1918, when British pilots training for the Great War were complemented by a squadron of American flyers. In the Second World War it was used as a Battle of Britain fighter station, before being transferred in 1943 to the 78th Fighter Group, who, by the cessation of hostilities, had flown over 450 missions. After the war, the airfield fell into disuse, before being renovated in the 1960s to accommodate several separate historic aircraft collections. Fifteen years ago, it became clear that the fragile and aged aircraft, donated by the USAF, needed shelter; standing out of their element in the inclement East Anglian

Robert Delaunay, *Propellers and Rhythm* (1937).

climate, it seemed that they were being abandoned to another, the earth. The building Foster proposed, and which was eventually built after an injection of Lottery money, was an elaboration of the basic hangar as well as a monumental tribute to the machinery it shelters.[50]

Placed at the edge of the airfield, the building is a huge glass façaded shell-like structure thrusting out from a turfed grassy mound. The visitor gains entrance through a tunnel in the earthworks, obviously meant to recall the reinforced shelters in airfields. Immediately inside the museum, one finds oneself on a platform

The interior of Norman Foster's American Air Museum at Duxford, Cambridgeshire, completed in 1997. The glass facade is removable so that aircraft on display can be taken in and out.

looking straight into the nose of the collection's B-52 Stratofortress, pristine and lethal. Clearly, the building's design was driven mainly by the need to house such a massive aircraft: the museum is 90 m (300 ft) long and elliptical on plan, like the flight path of Yeager's Starfighter, and, at its greatest, the free-spanning arch of the roof measures 82 m (270 ft) across and 20 m (65 ft) in height. However, the building's form was also determined by the desire to suspend some of the smaller aircraft, weighing up to 10 tonnes, from the roof, whose 'monocoque' concept is clearly derived from the stressed skin structure commonly employed in the construction of the aircraft themselves. Hence, overhead, is suspended a U-2 surveying everything that passes below its nose. To right and left, a ramp following the edge of the roof curves down to the ground, its bend dynamically opposed to the buttress-like walls enclosing the rear of the main hall. From this ramp, access to the exhibits is open: visitors are free to wander around, to crawl under wheel arches, to touch the aircraft, and imagine them in flight. For while these objects seem static, and some are highly strung, the fact that the glass façade of the museum is demountable means that the collection is never permanent. Most of the aircraft can be taken out into the open and, those still airworthy, returned to their element, beyond the clouds.

Yet there is, of course, an ever greater poignancy when war machines are displayed beyond exhibition spaces; mounted in environments as a reminder of how such aircraft can make the sky fall in. Consider May Bay B-52 ('B-52 Lake'), which the visitor can find in an obscure residential neighbourhood near Bach Thao Park, in Hanoi, Vietnam. About the size of a large swimming pool, this water-filled crater still holds wreckage from a B-52, one of fifteen shot down over the city in December 1972 during 'Operation Linebacker'. Shattered by the blast of a surface-to-air missile, and its resultant plunge, a length of fuselage, thirty years on still painted a military green and bearing the white stencilled letters spelling out United States Air Force, glowers in the heat. A forlorn set of main landing-gear wheels suggests how massive the aircraft must have seemed as it dropped out of the clouds that winter night, while the greenish-yellow hue of the stagnant pond suggests that hydraulic poisons continue to leak from the downed plane into the water supply. Though the lake is surrounded by a concrete walkway and cordoned off with railings, the Vietnamese authorities offer no details as to its significance; but in this case, perhaps, captions are redundant. All that might be claimed, neutrally, is that the suppurating pile of scrap metal somehow exhibits the fragile potency of a model aircraft in a way that the objects contained in dedicated aircraft museums so rarely do.

References

Preface

1 Marcel Proust, *The Prisoner*, translated and with an introduction by Carol Clark (London, 2002) p. 145.
2 Robin McKie, '100 years on, science still can't get Kitty Hawk to fly', *The Observer*, 23 March 2003, p. 29
3 Le Corbusier, *Aircraft* (London, 1935), p. 13.
4 *The Prisoner*, p. 661

1 Flight Engineering

1 It is reported that Chavez's last words, 'whose meaning cannot be interpreted, were: *Non, non, je ne meurs pas ... meurs pas.*' See John Berger, *G* (London, 1972), p. 209.
2 'Quando volai per la prima volta coll'aviatore Bielovucic, io sentii il petto aprirsi come un gran buco ove tutto l'azzurro del cielo deliziosamente s'ingolfava liscio fresco e torrenziale. Alla sensualità lenta stemperata, delle passeggiate nel sole e nei fiori, dovete preferire il massaggio feroce e colorante del vento impazzito.' F. T. Marinetti, *Teoria e invenzione futurista*, ed. Luciano De Maria (Milan, 1968), p. 116.
3 'Ecco che cosa mi disse l'elica turbinante, mentre filavo a duecento metri sopra i possenti fumaiuoli di Milano. E l'elica soggiunse . . . ' Marinetti, *Teoria e invenzione futurista*, p. 41.
4 'N'est-ce pas une âme en effet cet infiniment petit par rapport à l'ensemble de l'avion, par son imponderabilité même quand elle tourne à des folles vitesses, par sa fonction quand elle passe invisible dans l'éther azuré? Âme par sa contexture même, car elle exhale souvent sa vie dans un heurt délicat, maintes fois elle expire dans une caresse.' Lucien Chauvière, 'La Construction de l'hélice', in his *L'aéronautique pendant la Guerre Mondiale* (Paris, 1919), p. 198.
5 Jeffrey T. Schnapp, 'Propeller Talk', *Modernism/Modernity*, I/3 (1994), pp. 153–78.

I am much indebted to Professor Schnapp's work on Marinetti and the culture of flight.

6 'J'ai pu enfin attacher le bourdonnement à sa cause, à ce petit insecte qui trépidait là-haut, sans doute à bien deux milles mètres de hauteur; je le voyais bruire.' Marcel Proust, À la recherche du temps perdu, ed. Jean-Yves Tadié (Paris, 1999) p. 1908.

7 Dora Vallier, 'La Vie fait l'oeuvre de Fernand Léger', Cahiers d'Art, XXIX/2 (1954), pp. 133–72 (p. 140).

8 John Wright, 'Aeroplanes and Airships in Libya, 1911–1912', Maghreb Review, III (1978).

9 Le Corbusier, Aircraft (London, 1935) p. 9.

10 Ibid., p. 9.

11 Ibid., p. 10.

12 Harry Crosby, Shadows of the Sun, ed. Edward Germain (Santa Barbara, CA, 1977), p. 146.

13 George Buchanan Fife, Lindbergh (New York, 1927), p. 179.

14 Cited in John W. Ward, 'The Meaning of Lindbergh's Flight', American Quarterly, X/1 (Spring 1958), pp. 3–16.

15 Ibid., p.13.

16 Bertolt Brecht, Collected Plays: Three, ed. John Willett (London, 1997) p. 7.

17 See Stacy Schiff, Saint-Exupéry: a Biography (New York, 1994).

18 Antoine de Saint-Exupéry, Wind, Sand, and Stars, trans. and ed. William Rees (Harmondsworth, 1995), p. 32.

19 Gregory Corso, 'Flight', from Long Live Man (San Francisco, 1962).

20 Curtis Cate, Antoine de Saint-Exupéry: his Life and Time (London, 1970).

21 James Gilbert, The World's Worst Aircraft (London, 1975). See also Keith Sherwin, Man Powered Flight (Hemel Hempstead, 1971).

22 Ovid, Metamorphoses, Book viii, trans. Arthur Golding (London, 1567)

23 I owe these illustrations to Tom D Crouch, 'Kill Devil Hills, 17 December 1903', Technology and Culture, XL/3 (1999), pp. 595–8.

24 My account of the development of the Wright Flyer is indebted to Tom Crouch's magisterial survey of early flight in the US, A Dream of Wings: Americans and the Airplane 1875–1905. See also Roger E Bilstein, 'The Airplane, the Wrights, and the American Public', in The Wright Brothers: Heirs of Prometheus, ed. Richard P. Hallion (Washington, DC, 1978), pp. 39–51.

25 Hart Crane, 'Cape Hatteras', part 4 of The Bridge [1930], in Complete Poems, ed. Brom Weber (Newcastle upon Tyne, 1984), p. 86.

26 Paul Giles, Hart Crane: The Contexts of The Bridge (Cambridge, 1986), p. 114.

27 John Dos Passos, The Big Money (New York, 1936).

28 Geoffrey de Havilland, Sky Fever (London, 1961), p. 47.

29 'Experimental Trip of the Aeriel Machine', The Times, 25 April 1843, p. 9. The paper printed a retraction of this 'April Fool jeu d'esprit' on 29 April.

30 My account of Henson is indebted to E. Charles Vivian, A History of Aeronautics

(London, 1921) and Charles Gibb-Smith, *Aeronautics: Early Flying up to the Reims Meeting* (London, 1966).

31 Graham Wallace, *Flying Witness* (London, 1958), p. 44. See also Michael Paris, *Winged Warfare: the Literature and Theory of Aerial Warfare in Britain 1859–1917* (Manchester, 1992), p. 25.

32 Jules Verne, *Clipper of the Clouds* (London, 1887).

33 De Havilland, *Sky Fever*, p. 46.

34 Cited in Andrew Martin, *The Mask of the Prophet: the Extraordinary Fictions of Jules Verne* (Oxford, 1990), p. 159.

35 Norman Bel Geddes, *Horizons* (New York, 1933), pp. 109–21.

36 Le Corbusier, *Aircraft*, p. 74.

37 Bill Chaitkin, 'Not so Much an Aeroplane, More a Product Designer's Icon', *Design News* (1983); Tom Paulin, 'The Battle of Britain' in *The Invasion Handbook* (London, 2001), p. 182.

38 This account is indebted to Gary Hyland and Anton Gill, *The Last Talons of the Eagle* (London, 1998), pp. 156–62.

39 René Magritte, letter to André Breton, 24 June 1946.

40 Robert Melville, 'Exhibitions: Painting', *Architectural Review* (December 1961), p. 425.

41 H. J. Penrose, *British Aviation: the Adventuring Years 1920–29* (London, 1973).

42 The standard account of the Junkers aircraft firm is Richard Blunck, *Hugo Junkers: ein Leben für Technik und Luftfahrt* (Düsseldorf, 1951). In due course, Junkers also became involved in architectural fabrication for the Bauhaus. See Mirko Baum, *Hugo Junkers und das Bauhaus Dessau. Eine vergessene Episode aus der Geschichte des industrialisierten Bauens*, Konstruktives Entwerfen No.3, Werkbericht 2000, ed. M. Baum (Aachen, 2000).

43 De Havilland, *Sky Fever*, p. 13.

44 De Havilland, *Sky Fever*, p. 119; Peter King, *Knights of the Air* (London, 1988), p. 221.

45 De Havilland, *Sky Fever*, p. 226.

46 Quoted in King, *Knights of the Air*, p. 420.

47 *Ibid.*, p. 348.

48 Harold Mansfield, *Vision: the Story of Boeing* (New York, 1966), p. 151.

49 Douglas J. Ingells, *747: the Story of the Boeing Superjet* (New York, 1970).

2 Conquests of the Air

1 Bertolt Brecht, *Journals*, ed. John Willett, trans. Hugh Rorrison (London, 1993), p. 94.

2 Adolf Hitler, *Reden und Proklamationen, 1932–1945*, ed. Max Domarus (Neustadt, 1962).

3 Le Corbusier, *Aircraft* (London, 1935), p. 76.

4 H. G. Wells, 'The Argonauts of the Air' [1895], in *Selected Short Stories* (Harmondsworth, 1973), p. 219. The short story, recounting the first of all success-ful flights, ends with the craft crashing down onto the precincts of Imperial College, South Kensington, and onto the heads of those sceptical young scientists who claimed that the contraption would never leave the ground.

5 H. G. Wells, *The War in the Air* (London, 1908), p. 206. For absorbing accounts of Wells's apocalyptic fiction, see Robert Wohl, *A Passion for Wings: Aviation and the Western Imagination 1908-1918* (New Haven, CT, 1994), chapter 3; and Michael Paris, *Winged Warfare: the Literature and Theory of Aerial Warfare in Britain 1859-1917* (Manchester, 1992), chapter 2.

6 H. G. Wells, *The Outline of History* (New York, 1920), pp. 1084-5, quoting the Royal United Service Institution's Sir Louis Jackson.

7 Cited in Andrew Boyle, *Trenchard* (London, 1962), pp. 576-7. See also H. R. Allen, *The Legacy of Lord Trenchard* (London, 1972).

8 B. H. Liddell-Hart, quoted in Russell Weigley, *The American Way of War* (New York, 1973), p. 236.

9 Giulio Douhet, *The Command of the Air*, trans. Dino Ferrari (London, 1943).

10 Stanley Baldwin, House of Commons Debates, vol. 270, cols 631-2, 10 November 1932.

11 See Malcolm Smith, *British Air Strategy between the Wars* (Oxford, 1984); Uri Bialer, *The Shadow of the Bomber: the Fear of Air Attack and British Politics 1932-1939* (London, 1980); and Robert H. Ferrell, *Peace in Their Time: the Origins of the Kellogg-Briand Pact* (New Haven, CT, 1952).

12 Le Corbusier, *Aircraft*, pp. 83-4.

13 H. G. Wells, *The Shape of Things to Come: the Ultimate Revolution* (London, 1933), pp. 63, 216, 331.

14 Cited in Christopher Frayling, *Things to Come* (London, 1995), p. 58. For other accounts of the film, see Timothy Travers, 'The Shape of Things to Come: H. G. Wells and Radical Culture in the 1930s', *Film and History*, VI/2 (May 1976), pp. 31-6; and Paola Antonelli, 'Things to Come: La Transparenza del futuro', *Domus*, 719 (September 1990), pp. 90-97.

15 Cited in Frayling, p. 50.

16 T. E. Lawrence, *The Mint* (London, 1955), p. 181.

17 T. E. Lawrence, *The Seven Pillars of Wisdom* (London, 1935), p. 619.

18 Cited in David Killingray, '"A Swift Agent of Government": Air Power in British Colonial Africa', *Journal of African History*, XXV (1984), pp. 429-44 (p. 430).

19 The standard account of British air police work is David Omissi, *Air Power and Colonial Control: the Royal Air Force 1919-1939* (Manchester, 1990); but see also Hilary St George Saunders, *Per ardua: the Rise of British Air Power 1911-1939* (Oxford, 1945); and Viscount Templewood, *Empire of the Air* (London, 1957).

20 Le Corbusier, *Aircraft*, p. 12.

21 On the 'Aerial Odyssey', see Claudio G. Segre, *Italo Balbo: a Fascist Life* (Berkeley, CA, 1987).

22 Antoine de Saint-Exupéry, 'La fin tragique du "Maxime-Gorki"', in *Un sens à la vie*, ed. Claude Reynal (Paris, 1956), pp. 64–8. My account of the *Maxim Gorki* is based on Heinz Nowarra and G. R. Duval, *Russian Civil and Military Aircraft 1884–1969* (London, 1970); and James Gilbert, *The World's Worst Aircraft* (London, 1975), pp. 95–101. For the political background, see 'Technology and Legitimacy: Soviet Aviation and Stalinism in the 1930s', *Technology and Culture*, V (1976), pp. 55–81, and Scott W. Palmer, 'Peasants into Pilots: Soviet Air-mindedness as an Ideology of Dominance', *Technology and Culture*, XLI (2000), pp. 1–26.

23 Le Corbusier, *Aircraft*, p. 24.

24 For a contemporary account of the importance of the Ju-52, see Fischer von Porturzyn, ed., *Junkers and die Weltluftfahrt: Ein Beitrag zur Entstehungsgeschichte deutscher Luftgeltung, 1909–1934* (Munich, 1935). See also Edward Homze, *Arming the Lufwaffe: the Reich Air Ministry and the German Aircraft Industry 1919–1939* (Lincoln, NE, 1976); and John H. Morrow, 'Connections between Military and Commercial Aviation in Germany: Junkers, Heinkel, Dornier, through the 1930s', in *From Airships to Airbus: The History of Civil and Commercial Aviation*, ed. William F. Trimble, 2 vols (Washington, DC, 1995), II, pp. 152–67.

25 For political background to *Zauberfeuer*, see Eugene Emme, 'The Emergence of Nazi Luftpolitik as a Weapon in International Affairs', *Air Power Historian*, XII (1965), pp. 92–105; and Gabriel Jackson, *The Spanish Republic and the Civil War, 1931–39* (Princeton, NJ, 1965).

26 See John H. Morrow, *op. cit.*

27 My account of the destruction of Gernika draws on Gordon Thomas and Max Morgan Witts, *Guernica: the Crucible of World War II* (New York, 1975); and David Nevin, *Architects of Air Power* (Alexandria, VA, 1981), chapter 5.

28 George Steer, *The Tree of Gernika: a Field Study of Modern War* (London, 1938).

29 On dive-bombing techniques, see Hans-Ulrich Rudel, *Stuka Pilot*, trans. Lynton Hudson (Maidstone, 1973).

30 The phrase is George Barker's, from his 'Elegy on Spain', subtitled 'Dedication to the photograph of a child killed in an air raid on Barcelona', and first published in his collection *Lament and Triumph* (1940).

31 The chorus of Stuka pilots is quoted in David Welch, *Propaganda and the German Cinema 1933–1945* (Oxford, 1983), p. 214; H. K. Smith, *Last Train from Berlin* (London, 1943), p. 134.

32 Nevin, *Architects of Air Power*, p. 120.

33 On Churchill and Roosevelt in Quebec, see John Gunther, *Taken at the Flood: the Story of Albert D. Lasker* (New York, 1960), pp. 281–6. On de Seversky, see Phillip S Meilinger, 'Proselytiser and Prophet: Alexander P de Seversky and American Air Power', in John Gooch, ed., *Airpower: Theory and Practice* (London, 1995). On Disney's involvement in the war effort, see Alexander P. de Seversky, 'Walt Disney: an Airman in his Heart', *Aerospace Historian* (Spring 1967), p. 7; Richard Shale, *Donald Duck Joins Up* (Ann Arbor, 1982); and Walton Rawls, *Disney Dons*

Dog Tags (New York, 1992). Perhaps mention should also be made of the cartoon headline that appears at the climax of Disney's most successful wartime film: 'Dumbombers for Defense' (I owe this point to Mark Rawlinson).

34 James Agee, *The Nation*, 3 July 1943. For a useful account of the film, see Michael Paris, *From the Wright Brothers to Top Gun: Aviation, Nationalism and Popular Cinema* (Manchester, 1995), pp. 153–4.

35 On the various stages of the American bombing capability, see Robert W. Krauskopf, 'The Army and the Strategic Bomber, 1930–1939', *Military Affairs*, XXII (Summer 1958), pp. 83–94, 208–15; Kent Roberts Greenfield, *American Strategy in World War II: a Reconsideration* (Baltimore, 1963); Edward Jablonski, *America in the Air War* (Alexandria, VA, 1982); Ronald Schaffer, *Wings of Judgement* (New York, 1985); and Michael Sherry, *The Rise of American Air Power* (New Haven, CT, 1987).

36 Quoted in Kenneth P. Werrell, *Blankets of Fire: US Bombers over Japan during World War II* (Washington, DC, 1996), p. 216. My account of the Nagasaki bomb is indebted to Werrell's version of the raid.

37 On the B-36, see Michael Brown, *Flying Blind: the Politics of the US Strategic Bomber Program* (Ithaca, NY, 1992); Daniel Ford, 'B-36: Bomber at the Crossroads', *Air & Space* (April/May 1996). Contemporary ideas about US bomber policy are expressed in Thomas K. Finletter, *Survival in the Air Age* (Washington, DC, 1948); and Eugene M. Emme, ed., *The Impact of Air Power: National Security and World Politics* (New York, 1959).

38 Peter George, *Dr Strangelove, or How I Learned to Stop Worrying and Love the Bomb* (London, 1963). For a valuable account of the jet, see Jeffrey Ethell and Joe Christy, *B-52 Stratofortress* (New York, 1981).

39 See Vincent LoBrutto, *Stanley Kubrick* (London, 1997), p. 241.

40 June Jordan, 'To My Sister, Ethel Ennis, Who Sang "The Star-Spangled Banner" At The Second Inauguration Of Richard Milhous Nixon, January 20, 1973', from *Things That I Do In The Dark* (New York, 1977).

41 On the use of heavy bombers in South-east Asia and beyond, see Carl Berger, ed., *The United States Air Force in South East Asia, 1961–1973* (Washington, DC, 1977) and Bernard C Nalty *et al.*, *The Air War over Vietnam: Aircraft of the South East Asia Conflict* (New York, 1981).

42 Don de Lillo, *Libra* (New York, 1987), p. 80.

43 See James Nathan, 'A Fragile Détente: The U-2 Incident Re-examined', *Military Affairs*, XXXIX (1975), pp. 97–104.

44 Nicholson Baker, 'Model Aircraft', in *The Size of Thoughts: Essays and Other Lumber* (London, 1996), pp. 27–35.

45 For useful accounts of the B-2, see Richard Halloran, 'Stealth Bomber Takes Shape', *New York Times*, 16 May 1988; Rick Atkinson, 'Unravelling Stealth's Black World', *Washington Post*, 9 October 1989; and Brown, *Flying Blind*, pp. 294ff.

3 Silver Bullets

1 Cited in Christopher Frayling, *Things to Come* (London, 1995), p. 56.

2 *Flight Magazine*, 27 February 1926, cited in Frayling, *op. cit.*

3 Fred E. Weick and James R. Hansen, *From the Ground Up* (Washington, DC, 1988), pp. 66–7; see also George W. Gray, *Frontiers of Flight: the Story of NACA Research* (New York, 1948).

4 Walter Dorwin Teague, *Design This Day* (London, 1946), p. 143. The best account of the aircraft is Douglas J. Ingells, *The Plane that Changed the World: a Biography of the DC-3* (Fallbrook, CA, 1966); the role of aerodynamic research in this aircraft's evolution is documented in Richard P. Hallion, *Legacy of Flight: the Guggenheim Contribution to American Aviation* (Seattle, 1977).

5 Le Corbusier, *Aircraft* (London, 1935) [p. 40].

6 On the design and significance of this commission, see Daniele Pauly, *The Chapel at Ronchamp* (Basel, 1997), and Kenneth Frampton, *Le Corbusier* (London, 2001), pp. 167–76.

7 Le Corbusier, *Aircraft*, p. 50.

8 Le Corbusier, *Sketchbooks* (London, 1981), vol. III, sheet 637. Cf. 'The naval architect learns a great part of his lesson from the streamlining of a fish; the yachtsman learns that his sails are nothing more than a great bird's wing, causing the slender hull to fly along; and the mathematical study of the streamlines of a bird, and of the principles underlying the areas and curvatures of its wings and tail, has helped to lay the very foundations of the modern science of aeronautics.' Sir d'Arcy Wentworth Thompson, *On Growth and Form* (Cambridge, 1963), II, p. 941.

9 Cited in Rem Koolhaas, *Delirious New York* (London, 1978), p. 196.

10 J. G. Ballard, 'Project for a Glossary of the Twentieth Century', in *The User's Guide to the Millennium* (London, 1996), p. 277.

11 Cited in Peter Harry Brown and Pat H. Broeske, *Howard Hughes: the Untold Story* (London, 1996), p. 121. My account of Hughes's flight is based on this, and on Don Dwiggins, *Famous Fliers and the Ships They Flew* (New York, 1969).

12 Paul Virilio, *The Aesthetics of Disappearance* [1980], trans. Philip Beitchmann (New York, 1991), p. 25.

13 Armand van Ishoven, *Messerschmitt* (London, 1973), p. 95.

14 *Ibid.*, p. 104.

15 See C. F. Andrews and E. B. Morgan, *Supermarine Aircraft since 1914* (London, 1987), pp. 204–9.

16 Richard Hillary, *The Last Enemy* (London, 1942), p. 44. For a brilliant account of the importance of the 'myth' of Hillary, see Mark Rawlinson, *British Writing of the Second World War* (Oxford, 2000), pp. 39–67.

17 Andrews & Morgan, *Supermarine Aircraft*, p. 217. The standard account of the Spitfire's development is Eric B. Morgan and Edward Shacklady, *Spitfire: the History* (London, 2001); while the best biography of its designer is that written by his son, Gordon Mitchell, *R. J. Mitchell: Schooldays to Spitfire* (London, 2002).

18 Harald Penrose, *British Aviation: the Ominous Skies 1935–1939* (London, 1980), p. 69.

19 Kevin Brownlow, *David Lean* (London, 1995), p. 285. For a useful account of the film, see Michael Paris, *From the Wright Brothers to Top Gun: Aviation, Nationalism and Popular Cinema* (Manchester, 1995).

20 On Rattigan's wartime service in the RAF, see Michael Darlow and Gillian Hodson, *Terence Rattigan: the Man and his Work* (London, 1979), pp. 101–37. In fact, the test pilots about whom Rattigan was now writing for Lean were 'quiet young men absolutely unlike the types I had known during the war', p. 195.

21 The line is spoken by Ann Todd, then wife of the director.

22 Sir Geoffrey de Havilland, *Sky Fever* (London, 1961), p. 175.

23 Tom Wolfe, *The Right Stuff* (London, 1980), p. 61.

24 Mano Ziegler, *Rocket Fighter* (London, 1963), p. 63. Ziegler was a Luftwaffe test pilot who survived the Komet to tell its tale.

25 De Havilland, *Sky Fever*, p. 170.

26 Brownlow, *David Lean*, p. 294.

27 De Havilland, *Sky Fever,* p. 175.

28 Brownlow, *David Lean*, p. 295.

29 Chuck Yeager, *Yeager* (London, 1986), pp. 220–21. General background can be found in Richard P. Hallion, *Test Pilots: the Frontiersmen of Flight* (New York, 1981); on the X-1 and other supersonic projects following, see Richard P. Hallion, *Supersonic Flight: Breaking the Sound Barrier and Beyond* (New York, 1972).

30 Wolfe, *The Right Stuff*, p. 55.

31 Yeager, *Yeager*, pp. 154, 177.

32 J. H. Prynne, 'The Ideal Starfighter', *Poems* (Newcastle, 1998), p. 166.

33 Wolfe, *The Right Stuff*, p. 422.

34 Yeager, *Yeager*, p. 371

35 C. M. Sharp, *DH* (London, 1960), p. 302.

36 Roland Barthes, 'The Jet-Man', *Mythologies* (London, 1973), pp. 71–3.

37 For a detailed account of the procurement of the B-70, see Michael Brown, *Flying Blind: the Politics of the US Strategic Bomber Programme* (Ithaca, NY, 1992).

38 Cited in Douglas J. Ingells, *747: Story of the Boeing Super Jet* (Fallbrook, CA, 1970), p. 264.

39 Paul Virilio, *Pure War*, trans. Mark Polizotti (New York, 1997), p. 51. For balanced accounts of the politics of the SST, see Joshua Rosenbloom, 'The Politics of the American SST Programme: Origin, Opposition and Termination', *Social Studies of Science*, XI/4 (Nov 1981), pp. 403–23, and Mary E. Ames, *Outcome Uncertain: Science and the Political Process* (Washington, DC, 1978), pp. 49–82.

40 Jock Lowe, 'The Development of Concorde', Institute of Contemporary British History seminar, 19 November 1998.
See http://www.icbh.ac.uk/seminars/concorde.html.

4 Model Planes

1 Ian Sinclair, *Crash* (London, 1999), p. 48.

2 W. H. Auden, 'The Orators', in *The English Auden*, ed. E. Mendelson (London, 1981).

3 T. E. Lawrence, *The Mint* (London, 1955), p. 203.

4 Paul Nash, 'The Personality of Planes', originally published in *Vogue* (March 1942); subsequently collected in *Outline: an Autobiography and Other Writings* (London, 1949), pp. 248–53.

5 Paul Nash, 'Bomber's Lair', *Outline*, pp. 254–57.

6 Nash, 'The Personality of Planes', p. 250. On the Whitley, see Oliver Tapper, *Armstrong-Whitworth Aircraft since 1913* (London, 1976).

7 William Blake, *Complete Writings*, ed. Geoffrey Keynes (Oxford, 1966), p. 683.

8 Nash, 'The Personality of Planes', p. 249.

9 On the Hampden, see C. H. Barnes, *Handley-Page Aircraft since 1907* (London, 1976)

10 Nash, 'Bomber's Lair', p. 256.

11 *Hamlet*, III.ii.369–70.

12 On the Wellington, see C. F. Andrews and E. B. Morgan, *Vickers Aircraft since 1908* (London, 1975)

13 The script of *The Way to the Stars* was written by Terence Rattigan, who would later provide the screenplay for *The Sound Barrier*. For a useful account of the film, see Anthony Aldgate and Jeffrey Richards, *Britain Can Take It: British Cinema in the Second World War* (Oxford, 1986). On the Blenheim, see C. H. Barnes, *Bristol Aircraft since 1910* (London, 1988).

14 Letter to Ruth Clark, late 1940/early 1941, cited in Anthony Bertram, *Paul Nash: the Portrait of an Artist* (London, 1955), pp. 271–80 (p. 274).

15 My account of the *Letatlin* is based on John Milner, *Vladimir Tatlin and the Russian Avant-garde* (London, 1983).

16 See John Thompson's description of the artist's work in his *Panamarenko* (London, 2000), p. 29.

17 Nicholson Baker, 'Model Aircraft', in *The Size of Thoughts: Essays and Other Lumber* (London, 1996), pp. 27–35.

18 Norman Bel Geddes, *Horizons* (New York, 1933), p. 10.

19 Hiram Maxim, *Natural and Artificial Flight* (London, 1908). My account of Maxim is indebted to Peter King, *Knights of the Air* (London, 1988), p. 24–5.

20 My account of the Do-X is indebted to Bill Gunston's article in *Aeroplane Monthly* (September 1973), and James Gilbert, *The World's Worst Aircraft* (London, 1975), pp. 101–9.

21 My account of the Brabazon is indebted to Bill Gunston, 'Mighty Brabazon', *Aeroplane Monthly* (June 1974); C. H. Barnes, *Bristol Aircraft since 1910* (London, 1988); and Robert Wall, *Brabazon: the World's First Jumbo Airliner* (Bristol, 1999).

22 Norman Foster, 'Taking Flight', in *On Foster . . . Foster On*, ed. David Jenkins (Munich, 2000), p. 620.

23 Norman Foster, 'Building Sights: Boeing 747', in *On Foster . . . Foster On*, p. 589.

24 Clive James, *Flying Visits* (London, 1984) p. 8.

25 Norman Foster, 'Building Sights: Boeing 747', p. 590.

26 Norman Foster, 'On Flying', in *On Foster . . . Foster On*, pp. 685–93. The architects of flight featured on the stamps were: Reginald J. Mitchell (1895–1937), of Supermarine; Sydney Camm (1893–1966), designer of the Hawker Hurricane; George Carter (1889–1969) of the Gloster Aircraft Company, who worked with Frank Whittle (the designer of the jet engine) to create the Meteor; Roy Chadwick (1893–1947) of Avro, who was responsible for the design of the Lancaster bomber; Ronald Bishop (1903–1989), head of design for de Havilland and responsible for the all-wooden Mosquito, and later the Comet jet airliner.

27 Reyner Banham, 'Introduction', *Foster Associates* (London, 1979), pp. 4–8.

28 Quoted in Martin Pawley, 'The Last of the Piston Engine Men', *Building Design* (1 October 1971), p. 6.

29 Reyner Banham, 'Big Doug, Small Piece', *Architect's Journal*, CXXXVI (1 August 1962), pp. 251–3.

30 *Ibid.*

31 On Loewy's contribution to United Airlines, see John Zukowsky, 'Introduction', *Building for Air Travel*, ed. J. Zukowsky (Munich, 1996), p. 25.

32 Reyner Banham, 'Big Doug, Small Piece', p. 252.

33 Le Corbusier, *Sketchbooks*, IV: *1957–64* (New York, 1982), fiche 787.

34 Le Corbusier-Saugnier, 'Les Maisons "Voisins"', *L'Ésprit nouveau*, no. 2, p. 214. Quoted by Reyner Banham, *Theory and Design in the First Machine Age* (Oxford, 1960), p. 222. Saugnier is the pseudonym used by Ozenfant when writing about architecture in *L'Ésprit nouveau*, while Le Corbusier is the pseudonym initially chosen by Charles-Edouard Jeanneret for the same purpose. See also Stanislaus Von Moos, 'Le Corbusier und Gabriel Voisin', in von Moos and Chris Smeenk, eds, *Avantgarde und Industrie* (Delft, 1983), pp. 77–90.

35 Banham, *Theory and Design*, p. 222.

36 Le Corbusier, *Towards a New Architecture* (London, 1927), p. 100.

37 *Ibid.*, p. 102.

38 *Ibid.*, p. 105.

39 On Ader's achievements, see E. Charles Vivian, *A History of Aeronautics* (London, 1921) and Charles Gibb-Smith, *Aeronautics: Early Flying up to the Reims Meeting* (London, 1966).

40 Banham, *Theory and Design*, p. 242.

41 *Ibid.*, p. 242.

42 On Le Corbusier's use of advertising media in his own manifestos, see Beatriz Colomina, *Privacy and Publicity: Modern Architecture as Mass Media* (Cambridge, MA, 1994).

43 Le Corbusier, *Towards a New Architecture*, p. 106.

44 Kenneth Frampton, *Le Corbusier* (London, 2001), p. 77.

45 Le Corbusier, *Aircraft* (London, 1935), p. 13.

46 *Ibid.*, p. 31.

47 Kenneth Frampton, *Modern Architecture: a Critical History* (London, 1993), pp. 206–7. See also Marla Susan Stone, *The Patron State: Culture and Politics in Fascist Italy* (Princeton, 1998) pp. 223–6.

48 See Jean-Louis Cohen, 'Notre client est notre maître: Le Corbusier et Bat'a', *I clienti di Le Corbusier*, in *Rassegna*, no. 3 (July 1980), pp. 47–60.

49 On this pavilion, see Frampton, *Le Corbusier*, pp. 138–40.

50 For a good account of the building, see Penny McGuire, 'Flying Colours', *Architectural Review* (February 1997), pp. 52–6.

Select Bibliography

Anderton, David, *The History of the US Air Force* (London, 1981)

Andrew, C. F. and E. B. Morgan, *Vickers Aircraft since 1908* (London, 1988)

—, *Supermarine Aircraft since 1914* (London, 1981)

Balchin, Nigel, *The Aircraft Builders* (London 1947)

Barker, R., *The Schneider Trophy Races* (London, 197)

Barnes, C. H., *Bristol Aircraft since 1910* (London, 1964)

—, *Handley-Page Aircraft since 1907* (London, 1988)

—, *Shorts Aircraft since 1900* (London, 1988)

Beckles, C., *Birth of the Spitfire* (London, 1941)

Berg, A. Scott, *Lindbergh* (New York, 1998)

Bilstein, Roger E., *Flight in America: From the Wrights to the Astronauts* (Baltimore, 2001)

Bishop, Chris, *The Encyclopaedia of 20th-Century Air Warfare* (Leicester, 2001)

Bowyer, Chaz, *History of the RAF* (London, 1977)

Brabazon, Lord, *The Brabazon Story* (London, 1956)

Bright, Charles D., *The Jet Makers: The Aerospace Industry from 1945 to 1972* (Lawrence, KA, 1978)

Brooks, Peter W., *The Modern Airliner: Its Origins and Development* (London, 1961)

Ceruzzi, Paul, *Beyond the Limits: Flight Enters the Computer Age* (Cambridge, MA, 1989)

Collier, B., *A History of Air Power* (London, 1974)

Constant, Edward. W., *The Origins of the Turbojet Revolution* (Baltimore, 1980)

Crouch, Tom D., *A Dream of Wings: Americans and the Airplane* (New York, 2002)

Davies, R.E.G., *History of the World's Airlines* (London, 1964)

Davy, M.J.B., *Aeronautics: Heavier-than-Air Aircraft* (London, 1936)

—, *Interpretive History of Flight* (London, 1948)

De Havilland, Sir Geoffrey, *Sky Fever* (London, 1961)

Deighton, Len, *Bomber* (London, 1970)

Frater, Alexander, *Beyond the Blue Horizon* (London, 1986)

Gann, Ernest, *Fate Is the Hunter* (New York, 1961)

Gibbs-Smith, Charles H., *A History of Flying* (London, 1953)

—, *Aviation: An Historical Survey* (London, 1970)

—, *The Aeroplane* (London, 1960)

—, *The Rebirth of European Aviation* (London, 1974)

Gray, Peter and Owen Thetford, *German Aircraft of the First World War* (London, 1962),

Gunston, Bill, *The Jet Age* (London, 1971)

Hallion, Richard P., *On the Frontier: Flight Research at Dryden, 1946-1981* (Washington, DC, 1984)

—, *Test Pilots: The Frontiersmen of Flight* (Washington, DC, 1988)

Hart, Clive, *The Prehistory of Flight* (Berkeley, 1985)

Heppenheimer, T. A., *Turbulent Skies: The History of Commercial Aviation* (New York, 1995)

Higham, Robin, *Air Power: A Concise History* (London, 1972)

—, *Britain's Imperial Air Routes, 1918–39* (London, 1960)

Howard, Frank, *Wilbur and Orville* (London, 1988)

— and Bill Gunston, *The Conquest of the Air* (New York, 1972)

Hudson, Kenneth, *Air Travel: A Social History* (London, 1972)

— and Julian Pettifer, *Diamonds in the Sky* (London, 1979)

Hynes, Samuel, *Flights of Passage* (New York, 1988)

Ingells, Douglas J., *747: Story of the Boeing Super Jet* (Fallbrook, CA, 1970)

Jackson, A. J., *Avro Aircraft since 1908* (London, 1965)

—, *Blackburn Aircraft since 1909* (London, 1968)

—, *British Civil Aircraft, 1919–1959*, 3 vols (London, 1988)

—, *De Havilland Aircraft since 1909* (London, 1965)

James, D. N., *Gloster Aircraft since 1917* (London, 1987)

—, *Schneider Trophy Aircraft, 1913–31* (London, 1981)

Jones, H. A. and Sir Walter Raleigh, *The War in the Air*, 6 vols (London 1922–37)

Lewis, P., *British Aircraft 1809–1914* (London, 1962)

—, *The British Bomber since 1914* (London 1974)

—, *The British Fighter since 1912* (London, 1974)

Lindbergh, Charles, *The Spirit of St Louis* (New York, 1953)

Mansfield, Harold, *Vision: The Story of Boeing* (New York, 1966)

Mason, F. K., *Hawker Aircraft since 1920* (London, 1971)

Mitchell G., ed., *R. J. Mitchell* (London, 1986)

Montgomery Hyde, H., *British Air Policy Between the Wars, 1918–1939* (London, 1976)

Morpugo, J., *Barnes Wallis* (London 1972)

Morrow, John H., *The Great War in the Air: Military Aviation from 1909 to 1921* (Washington, DC, 1993)

Munson, Kenneth, *Airliners Between the Wars, 1919–1939* (New York, 1972)

Nevin, David, *Architects of Air Power* (Alexandria, VA, 1981)

Overy, R. J., *The Air War, 1939–45* (London, 1980)

Penrose, H., *Architect of Wings* (Shrewsbury, 1985)

—, *The Adventuring Years, 1920–29* (London, 1973)

—, *Widening Horizons, 1930–4* (London, 1979)

—, *Ominous Skies, 1935–9* (London, 1980)

Quill, J., *Spitfire: A Test Pilot's Story* (London, 1983)

Saunders, H., *Per Ardua: the Rise of British Air Power, 1911–39* (London, 1944)

Scott, J. D., *Vickers: A History* (London, 1964)

Serling, Robert J., *The Jet Age* (Alexandria, VA, 1982)

Smith, J. R. and Antony Kay, *German Aircraft of the Second World War* (London 1972),

Smith, M., *British Air Strategy Between the Wars* (Oxford, 1984)

Smith, Peter, *The History of Dive Bombing* (Annapolis, 1982)

Solberg, Carl, *Conquest of the Skies: A History of Commercial Aviation in America* (Boston, 1979)

Stewart, O., *Aviation: The Creative Ideas* (London, 1966)

Tapper, O., *Armstrong-Whitworth Aircraft since 1913* (London, 1973)

Swanborough, Gordon and Peter M. Bowers, *United States Navy Aircraft Since 1911* (Washington, DC, 1990)

—, *United States Military Aircraft Since 1909* (Washington, DC, 1989)

Taylor, J.W.R., *A History of Aerial Warfare* (London 1974)

Thetford, Owen, *Aircraft of the Royal Air Force since 1918* (London, 1988)

—, *British Naval Aircraft since 1912* (London, 1988)

Thompson, Milton O., *At the Edge of Space: The X-15 Flight Program* (Washington, DC, 1992)

Whittle, Sir Frank, *Jet: The Story of a Pioneer* (London 1954)

Wohl, Robert, *A Passion for Wings: Aviation and the Western Imagination, 1908–1918* (New Haven, 1994)

Wood, Derek and Derek Dempster, *The Narrow Margin: The Battle of Britain and the Rise of Airpower, 1930–40* (London, 1961)

Acknowledgements

I am grateful to the following for help, advice, insights, support, and encouragement during the writing of this book: Spilios Argyropoulous, Susan Castillo, Jon Clark, Vivian Constantinopoulos, John Coyle, Harry Gilonis, Stephen Johnson, Joe Kerr, Vassiliki Kolocotroni, Michael Leaman, Jane Lewty, Aris Loupas, Paddy Lyons, Willy Maley, Andrew and Deborah Marsland, Rob Maslen, Jo McIvor, Donald MacKenzie, Adam and Diane Piette, Mark Rawlinson, Dizziana Rossi, Olga Taxidou and Irina von Wiese. Errors, infelicities and omissions are mine alone.

Photographic Acknowledgements

The author and publishers wish to express their thanks to the below sources of illustrative material and/or permission to reproduce it:

Photos © ADAGP, Paris and DACS, London 2003: pp. 16, 22, 51; photos from the author's collection: pp. 12, 187; photo courtesy BAE Systems plc: p. 148, 194, 195; photo courtesy of Blohm & Voss A.G.: p. 50; photos courtesy Boeing Company: p. 121, 198; photo, Charles E. Brown: p. 58; photo Richard Bryant/Arcaid: p. 218; La Chambre Claire, Neuchatel: p. 28; © DACS, 2003: p. 6; Dean Gallery, Edinburgh (photo: Scottish National Galleries): p. 51; Deutsches Museum, München: p. 57; photo courtesy of Fokker: p. 20; photos courtesy of the Fondation Le Corbusier: pp. 202, 209, 210, 213; photo courtesy Grumman-Northrop: p. 114; Hulton-Getty: p. 207 (foot); Imperial War Museum, London: pp. 77, 140; photos courtesy of the Italian Air Ministry: pp. 18, 80, 207 (top); Kelvingrove Art Gallery, Glasgow: p. 178; Kunstmuseum, Basel: p. 17; Kunstmuseum Wolfsburg (photo Helge Mundt): p. 180 (foot); Leeds City Art Gallery: p. 175; photo courtesy Lockheed Martin p. 130; photos courtesy Lufthansa: pp. 55, 65, 85, 86, 89, 191; photos courtesy Messerschmitt A.G.: pp. 96, 136, 147 (foot); Münchner Stadtmuseum (Puppentheatermuseum): p. 193; Musée National d'Art Moderne, Paris: p. 217; Musée National Fernand Léger, Biot: p. 16; Museo Storico dell'Aeronautica, Bracciano: p. 6; photos courtesy NASA: pp. 27, 31, 63, 64, 111, 115, 123, 151, 152, 154, 155, 158, 161, 163, 165; photo Novosti: p. 82; © Eduardo Paolozzi, 2003. All Rights Reserved, DACS: p. 193; photo courtesy of the RIBA, London: p. 59; photo courtesy the Russian State Archive for Literature and Art, Moscow: p. 180 (top); photo courtesy of Peter Sauerer: p. 183 (top); photo courtesy of the Smithsonian Institution, Washington, DC: p. 36; The Tate Archive (Nash 7050): p. 171; photo Ullstein Bilddienst: p. 92; photo courtesy United Airlines: p. 201; photos courtesy USAF: pp. 10, 94, 99, 102, 104, 105, 116, 159, 183 (foot), 186; photos courtesy Vickers plc: pp. 49, 60, 137, 145; photo courtesy Whitford and Hughes, London: p. 61.

Index